JOHN PHILIP

SOUSA

Also by Ann M. Lingg

MOZART

JOHN PHILIP
SOUSA

by Ann M. Lingg

HOLT, RINEHART AND WINSTON
NEW YORK · CHICAGO · SAN FRANCISCO

In Canada, Holt, Rinehart and Winston of Canada, Limited.

Library of Congress Catalog Card Number: 54–5451

Published, October, 1954
Second Printing, March, 1955
Third Printing, August, 1955
Fourth Printing, October, 1959
Fifth Printing, August, 1963
Sixth Printing, October, 1965

The author has quoted from *Marching Along*, by John P. Sousa, with the kind permission of Charles T. Branford Company, Publishers, Boston, Massachusetts.

95267-0214
Printed in the United States of America

ACKNOWLEDGMENTS

The author is indebted to the following people for providing her with important material used in this book: Jane Priscilla Sousa; Helen Sousa Abert; John Philip Sousa, 3rd; J. W. Bell; Olin Downes; Dr. Edwin Franko Goldman; Emil Mix; Nicoline Zedeler Mix; Staff Sergeant Marjorie Moore, USMC; Lieutenant Colonel William F. Santelman, USMC; N. Waters.

JOHN PHILIP
SOUSA

prologue

The mourning flags came down and glorious symbols of victory sprouted along the streets of the nation's capital. Banners, garlands, evergreens, and streamers formed an undulating arch of triumph over Pennsylvania Avenue.

"Welcome to the Nation's Heroes!" inscriptions shouted. "Welcome to the Army of the Potomac!" "Welcome to the Gallant Fifth and Sheridan's Invincibles!" And, "To Greet All Who Fought, to Weep for All Who Fell!"

The date was May 24, 1865, and the Grand Review of the victorious Union Army marked the end of the Civil War.

Washington was bursting at the seams. A million soldiers were encamped, awaiting discharge. A fabulous number of patriots had rented every square foot from cellars to attics to witness the great march of victory. The day was still young, rosy with the first flush of dawn, as people trooped to grandstands, climbed house tops, lined sidewalks, to extend a passionate tribute to the 150,000 soldiers who would be marching, to the more than twice that number who had died of wounds and disease—and to the one man who had been murdered. Before their minds' eyes rose a shining shadow—the long, lean, awkward frame of Abraham Lincoln, symbol of union re-established in battle.

In front of the White House was a pavilion all covered with flags, roses, and evergreens. Here Andrew Johnson, the new President, and his military staff would review the troops. Grandstands for officials, dignitaries, and disabled veterans had been built on the other side of the avenue. Near the Capitol, where the parade would start, school-children waited, singing.

The girls were in white, the boys wore sailor pants and black jackets. They all had red white and blue rosettes pinned to their shirts. Some carried flowers. Unaware of the horrors of war, the children of Washington now enjoyed the pageant of its triumph.

A middle-aged man in a Marine Band uniform squeezed onto a platform near the presidential pavilion, herding two boys ahead of him. Antonio Sousa, a trombone player, was not on duty, but he had donned his uniform nevertheless and, of course, he had taken the boys along—his own son, John Philip, and his wife's nephew, Gus Lohr. Philip was eleven, a music student and a chum of practically every musician in the Marine Band. He knew every note in their repertory and sometimes they let him bang the cymbals, strike the triangle, or even blow into a huge horn. While Gus and the other boys were set on becoming streetcar conductors and wearing portable change-makers around their necks, Philip was determined to be a musician. This

2

was the first decision he had made, he couldn't remember now how long ago.

At nine o'clock a cannon shot signaled the beginning of the parade. The human surf fell instantly silent, but then a joyous "Hurrah" rang out. Bareheaded General Sherman approached the stand, followed by some members of his staff.

From down the avenue emerged faint martial sounds. They grew and swelled, and then a stream of soldiers came in sight. On a garlanded charger rode General Meade, leading the Army of the Potomac. As the splendid cavalcade passed the reviewing stand, guards presented arms; a deafening cheer rolled on like a wave, breaking with a roar as the general veered off and headed for his seat.

Hurrahs burst, exploded. The President of the United States had made his appearance, and with him was a general, his bearded face set in grave determination. "Grant! Grant! Hurrah for Grant!" the crowd acclaimed the man to whom General Lee had surrendered his sword. More officers and officials came up behind the two men. Two children were in the group.

"The Grant boys!" Gus said in awe.

"Must be mighty proud of their Dad," John Philip whispered back.

Bands blared, boots clamped, soldiers sang, handkerchiefs fluttered, streamers and flowers stirred in the breeze. *Rally round the flag . . . When Johnny comes marching home . . . Tramp, tramp, tramp, the boys are marchin'* . . . The surging sounds swept along with the troops, voices rising over the din of hoofs, sabers, and bugles—sidewalks and avenue one rolling stream of song.

3

People wept as they sang with the marchers; some ran into the streets and kissed the worn, torn flags. In a country virtually without a standing army, the largest armies that had seen action in modern times had been raised in a national emergency. And now those young men, their faces hardened and aged by the gruesome spectacle of bloodshed, were ready to put their arms away and to return to their peaceful professions, determined to see the banner under which they had fought wave over a nation undivided and indivisible, forever.

Regimental standards were lowered in salute as they were carried past the reviewing stand. Sheridan's cavalry clattered by; then came Burnside's Ninth Corps with its cannon-and-anchor shields; Merritt's men, and Parke's, and Griffin's, and Humphrey's. Then, suddenly, the crowd recoiled. A bolting horse raced up the avenue. The rider's cap had been blown away, and his long yellow hair and bright red scarf fluttered in the wind. "Custer!" someone yelled. Women shrieked. Philip grasped his father's arm in terror.

"It's Custer," Antonio Sousa said. "He'll manage."

A few breathless moments later the young general brought the foaming mount under control. Trotting back, he saluted smartly as he passed the presidential pavilion and joined his cavalry—rows of red scarves, carbines, and sabers, just coming up to the tunes of a band. On Custer's left arm still dangled the wreath that had been thrown at him and had frightened his horse.

All day they marched, bayonets glittering in the blazing sun, a surging wave of Union blue. Insignia and paraphernalia floated past—the Maltese crosses and clover leaves, the green-sprigged hats of the Irish, and the Zouaves' red-

4

tasseled caps. Cannons rumbled by; flower-adorned men, horses, and wagons rode over flower-bedecked roads.

Tramp, tramp, tramp, the boys are marchin' . . . Philip hummed as he and Father returned to their house near the Navy Yard. His feet ached from hours spent on tiptoe, but the song kept them marching. *Tramp, tramp, tramp* . . . strange how this melody forced you to walk in rhythm, he thought. For the fun of it he tried to fall out of step with himself, but the march was stronger than he.

Next day the Western troops were marching—General Sherman and his legendary frontiersmen. And then it was all over—war, as well as triumph. The Stars and Stripes, crowned with new glory, fluttered in the breeze under the bluest of skies.

chapter one

MARCH music always stayed with Philip, long after the last sound had vanished. It made him feel light and happy, it gave rhythm to his thoughts and motions; but never before had he felt such pride, and elation, and joy. No longer would those who played this music march off at the head of dark, long columns and be brought back, maimed, to hospitals and cemeteries. "War" now meant victory, exuberant crowds, jubilant songs, flowers, color, and radiant skies. People were saying many things about the country's future, which Philip could not understand; but the triumphant march tunes had struck new chords in his heart and mind.

Philip was born on November 6, 1854, the oldest boy of a flock of brothers and sisters that would eventually grow to ten. His father was a Spaniard of Portuguese ancestry who had gone to England as a youth, and later met his German bride in Brooklyn. Elizabeth Trinkhaus came from a small south German town of which her father had been the mayor. During the mid-forties, when people were restive and the breath of revolution was in the air, Mayor Trinkhaus had shipped his children to America, one by one.

Antonio Sousa's youth, too, had been affected by politics. Sousa was an old and distinguished name in Portugal; but in the 1820's one of that country's brisk revolutions, that came like a cloudburst in midsummer, had caught Antonio's father on the wrong side of the fence, and he and his bride barely escaped to Spain where she died in childbirth.

Antonio wasn't very communicative about his youth, but his children loved his story about how they owed their existence to a minor blaze in a small apartment somewhere in Spain. Antonio had been about 14 the night the candle toppled over. He was supposed to take care of his younger stepbrothers and stepsisters; but in his panic he had run away and kept on running until he got to the waterfront and hid in a ship. Exhausted, he fell asleep; and when he awoke he was en route to England. He never went back to Spain. How and where he acquired his fine education and how he eventually got to Brooklyn—all this remained shrouded in mystery.

One version has it that Antonio led the life of a seafaring band musician, playing under the flag of various nationalities until he alighted from an American man-of-war in the Brooklyn Navy Yard, to remain a landlubber ever after. His and Elizabeth's first child, Katherine ("Tinnie"), was born in Brooklyn. They moved to Washington shortly before John Philip's birth.

It seems that music was the least accomplishment of Antonio Sousa, even though he played the trombone for a living. His real love was literature. In this he followed in

7

the footsteps of a distinguished ancestor, Luis de Sousa, a Dominican monk and noted historian and writer who lived at the turn of the 17th century. John Philip Sousa's earliest memories of his father were that of a man sitting in the front yard behind a large reading stand on which four or five books were propped up—each in a different language.

His father, Sousa remembered later, was not particularly industrious but wonderfully handy at doing the things he liked. He was an expert at shooting and fishing—quite an asset in the Navy Yard where a boy's prestige depended on his prowess with gun and rod.

The Navy Yard, or "Pipetown" district, was one of several sections into which Washington was then divided, others being "Swamp Poodle," "Capitol Hill," "The Island," and "The Northern Liberties," where the rich lived. The town then consisted of a handful of scattered government buildings separated by muddy streets where geese and hogs promenaded; a couple of rows of embassies, large homes, and hotels; and wide stretches of malaria-breeding marshland which reached to the President's front door. The Treasury and Smithsonian Institute were completed, but the Washington Monument was as unfinished as the Capitol. Pennsylvania Avenue had sidewalks shaded by elms that Jefferson had planted, but along its southern rim were slums, markets, and an open sewer; and within earshot of the President slave auctions were held once a week. Connecticut Avenue got lost in junglelike woodland, and people went rabbit shooting right behind the new Willard Hotel. The living habits were still those of the South; country squires with broad-brimmed hats rode in fine carriages drawn by prancing horses; their Negro house slaves climbed stiffly from the boxes of coaches, opened carriage doors in front of fine houses, lounged on sidewalks while the master was indoors. Heavy horse-drawn buses, at twelve and a half cents a ride, rumbled down Pennsylvania Avenue, working havoc with its surface. The Sousa boys loved it all—this colorful pageant in a haphazardous little place dedicated to governing a country not yet a hundred years old.

From the small house between Sixth and Seventh avenues where John Philip was born, Antonio moved his family twice until in 1858 they finally landed in their own house on a 600-dollar lot, one third of which Antonio sold to Salvadore Accardi, a one-legged workman in the Navy Yard, whose son Ed became John Philip's chum. On the north side of the lot, facing E Street, Antonio built a little shack which he called "the shop," where he started to practice cabinetmaking, a trade he expected to support the family with, after his asthma would force him to abandon the trombone.

The side yard of the lot was the children's. Here John Philip experienced the delights and petty griefs of childhood. Here the neighborhood boys, who had no private playing ground, would assemble, which greatly enhanced Philip's popularity. Here he would sit for hours, listening to the faint sounds of band music which the wind carried over from the Marine Barracks nearby.

Philip was a rugged individualist at the age of four. And at five, he nearly killed himself to punish his mother. One evening, when his determined request for "just one more doughnut" was just as determinedly denied, he announced that Mother would be sorry, and stalked out in grave silence. It was raining hard, but he found a plank

9

in the side yard and "went to bed" outdoors. He heard his mother call him, but did not reply. He watched her frantic search, yet gave no sign. At long last she found him, a soaked and shivering bundle, half-unconscious from exposure and fear. His stubborn feat resulted in pneumonia, followed by dangerous complications and a latent illness of nearly two years.

He couldn't go to school. His sister Tinnie and Father taught him the fundamental rules of reading, writing, and arithmetic. Sometimes, during his confinement, he heard visitors whisper, "They'll never raise that boy," and then he felt sorry for himself without quite knowing why.

Then, one evening—he had been growing strong during the past month or so, but still felt weary—he felt a sudden, irrepressible desire to play baseball. He had no bat but found a ball and threw it with indomitable energy, utterly unconcerned over the safety of Signor and Signora Esputa, who were visiting his parents. Esputa was a neighbor who lived nearby in a large brick house on Eighth Street, and Antonio's favorite crony. He too had played with the Marines, until his retirement in 1859, and he too was from Spain.

"This boy ought to do something useful," Esputa grumbled. "I'll teach him some music."

"He's too young," Antonio said, "and not quite well yet."

"Couldn't be more active . . ."

Philip dropped the ball. "But I want to play music," he said, and pleaded with his father until Antonio finally gave in.

The first lesson was a nightmare. Esputa started with solfeggio, the old, time-honored *do-re-mi*. Philip was supposed to sing after him. But the old Spaniard had an awful voice. When excited he squeaked like a mouse; when calm he squawked like a crow. And whatever weird sounds he emitted, to Philip they sounded all alike.

"*Do*," the crow croaked.

"*Do*," Philip croaked obediently.

"No, *do*," whistled the mouse.

"*Do*," Philip squeaked bravely.

By then, Esputa was certain that the boy was making fun of him. Red in the face, he sputtered invectives and screamed he would discontinue the instruction—only to return the following day to squeak and squawk for a full hour, with Philip struggling after him. The Spaniard's screeching voice kept haunting Philip, yet it could not destroy his love of music.

By that summer Philip had fully recovered. At last he was able to get outdoors. On the embankment of the Anacostia River, near the present site of the Sousa Bridge, he and Gus would sit for hours and try to catch fish in the muddy waters; and they were mighty proud when some wretched small creature would take their bait. Sometimes his father would wake him at four o'clock in the morning and take him hunting in a hazy marshland still drowsy with night.

In the fall he went to school. Then one day Esputa's son John paid a visit and announced that he was opening a conservatory in the neighborhood; would the Sousas enroll Philip as a student?

"Even if he doesn't learn anything, it will at least keep him off the streets," he said.

There was good reason to keep a boy off the streets. War had been declared. Washington was an armed camp.

Barracks and hospitals sprang up in parks. Refugees squatted in open spaces. Soldiers camped in private gardens and under the half-finished dome of the Capitol. Negroes, groping their way North to the mysteries and hazards of freedom, built cabins in the surrounding woods. Battle sounds occasionally reverberated in the outskirts of the city.

In the Navy Yard households were fatherless for long stretches of time, and marauding soldiers broke into unprotected houses. Antonio Sousa, too, left with the Marines, and often the children saw their mother, white with fear, lead some staggering drunkard in uniform out their front door; and they would put down their homework while she prayed for their safety.

Yet, Philip resented the remark about having to be kept off the streets. He decided not to speak one unnecessary word to John Esputa although he didn't object to being enrolled in his class. He came on time, answered questions, played what he was asked to play, and left. They all thought he was dumb.

After three years, examinations were held. And a bewildered John Esputa called on Antonio Sousa and announced that Philip had won top honors in all of the five contests.

"What shall I do? I can't give them all to one and the same boy!" he exclaimed.

Antonio could afford to be generous. "Possession of the medals won't make him any smarter," he said with a characteristic Latin sense of drama, "and if you can make better use of them, by all means do."

They settled on three medals. Philip was so proud that he even forgot his grievances against his teacher. At home, he spread the three little golden lyres on the table, looked at them, touched them. No medal he would ever receive from kings or potentates would give him the feeling of accomplishment that the three golden lyres produced.

But only a year later antagonism flared up again. Philip was getting capricious and resented criticism. And John Esputa had contracted boils in parts of his anatomy that forced him to spend his days in a hammock. He was in great pain and in a very bad mood when Philip arrived for class one day. Esputa started to nag, finding fault with whatever his prize pupil did.

"Draw a long bow," he snapped.

"I'm drawing the bow as long as I can," Philip snapped back.

"Don't you dare contradict me!"

"My arm's already up against the wall . . ." Philip began, but the irate professor lashed out with a valuable violin bow. He tried to hit Philip, but hit the stove and broke the bow in two. "Get out of here before I kill you . . ." he yelled.

"I'll smash this fiddle over your head . . ." Philip shrieked.

Slamming out of the door, he raced home. Hit him! This wasn't the way a Sousa was brought up. It was disgraceful, shameful! Still shaking with fury, he told his father that he would never set foot in the conservatory again.

"I suppose you don't want to be a musician," Antonio said slowly. "What else would you want to do?"

Philip hadn't thought of that. Something easy, he thought, and looked helplessly out of the window. Some-

13

thing where he wouldn't be exposed to insult. A comforting smell of doughnuts came from the kitchen.

"I want to be a baker," he said.

"A baker?"

"Y—yes . . ."

"Well . . . I'll try to get you a job."

An hour later, at lunch, Father announced that Charlie, the baker two blocks down the street, had accepted Philip as an apprentice as of that very night. Of course, Father added, Philip would have to continue school. School in the morning, homework in the afternoon, the bakery at night, if this was all right with him.

"Yes," Philip said. Anything rather than music . . .

At 8:30 P.M. sharp, he reported for work. It was thrilling to be up at night, when all the other boys had to go to bed. Charlie, his wife, and their helpers went out of their way to be nice. They fed him fresh hot pie—at four o'clock in the morning! At dawn, after half an hour's catnap, he helped them load the wagon and deliver bread. It was fun to ride through the empty streets and to watch the horse stopping at the right front doors all by itself, like an intelligent human being.

At eight o'clock he went home, ate breakfast, and went to school. That afternoon he was a little listless, too tired even to play baseball. But he didn't complain and bravely returned to work. But weren't the folks at the bakery less pleasant than the day before? They drove him hard; they gave him no pie. And when he reached school again he nearly fell asleep.

And the third night was even worse. Charlie started nagging, even yelling, almost like Esputa. Around midnight the baby cried and they sent Philip upstairs to rock

the cradle; he was groggy with weariness . . . he bent over
. . . and then he started up, as if somebody had slapped
him. There stood the baker's wife, calling him nasty names,
and the baby was still crying. He went reeling home that
morning, nearly unconscious with fatigue. Vaguely he
heard Father tell Mother to let him sleep all day. And at
dinner, when Father asked him whether he still wanted to
be a baker, he emphatically insisted that he would rather
die.

"Then you'd better make up with Esputa and start your
music again," Father said dryly, suppressing a smile of
satisfaction with himself and with Charlie, his accomplice.

chapter two

SOMETIME toward the end of the Civil War, at a
benefit concert, a well-scrubbed boy of ten or
eleven, his pitch-black shock of hair neatly
combed to one side, stepped onto the stage and fiddled with
remarkable skill, completely at ease. John Philip Sousa
never knew stage fright. Soon after this debut, when

scheduled to play at the St. Elizabeth Asylum for the Insane, he pitched baseball until one hour before the concert; and because he couldn't find a clean white shirt, he borrowed one from his teacher, which, of course, was many sizes too large and had to be fastened by an intricate array of pins. As he played, the pins dropped from him like needles from a Christmas tree on New Year's Day. The shirt slowly unfolded to full size and began to slide until the audience was hilarious. Panicky, Philip withdrew in disorder and ran home, without even collecting the ice cream and cake which constituted his fee.

At the venerable age of 11, Philip decided to make his skills pay. He rounded up seven unemployed musicians, appointed himself leader, first violinist, and general manager, and canvassed dance halls and dancing schools. Soon he had his band fully booked. The dancers were amused to see the child directing a band of seven fully grown men, the string bass player a white-haired gentleman old enough to be his grandfather.

They were playing on Saturdays at Professor Sheldon's establishment when the seven men requested that Philip ask for a raise of two dollars per nose. Philip was satisfied with the fee he collected, but the men insisted on cashing in on their popularity while it lasted. So Philip braced himself and presented his demands to the professor.

"And what are you going to do if I say no?" Sheldon asked.

Philip, full of dignity, said that he would quit. Sheldon was sorry. So was Philip as he walked out. But next Saturday, when he peeped into the dance hall to see how Sheldon had solved the crisis, he found his seven men happily playing under a different leader.

Thus ended Sousa's first band.

Violin, orchestration, harmony, sight-reading; some cello and viola da gamba; a student chorus doing mostly English glees or simple four-part pieces which Esputa wrote himself: this was the conservatory.

At school Philip excelled in arithmetic, history, geography. Hannah Johnson, his teacher, awarded him prizes for exemplary conduct and punctuality.

At home Father taught him the trombone. But here Philip was not as clever a pupil as he was at the rod and gun. Pipetowners dubbed him the world's worst trombonist and claimed that his practicing depreciated the real estate value of the neighborhood.

But he made good progress on the violin.

On a hot morning in June, 1868, he was in the front parlor practicing one of the difficult Bériot concertos, when there was a knock at the door and a stranger walked in without waiting for an answer.

"I wanted to know who was playing," he said. "I've been listening outside." He sat down without ceremony. "You play very nicely," he continued. "Have you ever thought of joining a circus?"

"A circus? No . . ." Now he remembered the man; he had seen him hanging around the circus which was now in an empty lot two blocks away.

"I'm the bandleader of the circus," the stranger said. "I could get you in. Twelve dollars a week, and everything free."

Twelve dollars a week. . . . The circus band . . . "I'd like to very much," Philip said slowly. "But I don't think my father would let me."

Too bad, the bandleader said glibly. Of course, some

fathers were narrow-minded and didn't understand the bright future of boys traveling with a circus. But if Philip would leave Washington with them the following night, quite secretly, and after a couple of days write his father and tell him how wonderful everything was, he might, after all, not call him back.

It was a deal.

Philip was too perturbed to get back to his concerto. Why should he bother now? But he had to talk to someone. Thirty-six hours to kill!

Ed Accardi was playing outside.

"Did you see the man who just left our house?" Philip asked.

"Didn't look like much to me. Got your baseball bat?"

"Got more important things on my mind." A pause. Then, "Can you keep a secret?"

Ed nodded.

"I've got a job. A terrific job—traveling all over the country. When I return I'll be famous and rich . . ."

"Traveling? With whom?"

"With the circus—tomorrow night—but you mustn't tell anyone . . . promise."

Ed didn't really *tell* his mother. He just pestered her to let him join the circus until Mrs. Accardi began to ask questions, found out about Philip, and dashed over to Elizabeth Sousa to warn her.

The Sousas had a long talk that night, and they slept little. Shortly after sunrise Antonio left the house. But when he returned an hour later, he seemed happy and relieved. He walked determinedly up the stairs to Philip's bedroom.

Philip had been dreaming of beautiful ladies in

spangled tights on flying trapezes; of roaring lions and tigers; of buckets full of lemonade; and of himself conducting a band of a hundred giants, under a tent that reached up to the stars. "Good morning, son," Father's voice woke him. "Get up and put on your Sunday clothes."

This was quite unusual on an ordinary weekday, but everything was unusual today. His last day at home . . .

"Let's go out," Father said after breakfast.

Slowly they walked the two blocks to the Marine Barracks. They passed the gate, crossed the parade grounds, entered the Commandant's mansion.

General Zeilin sat behind a huge desk. "So this is our new apprentice?" he asked.

"Yes, sir."

"Welcome to the Marine Band, Philip!"

Philip felt his mouth open in overwhelming surprise. The Marine Band . . . The President's own band . . . He was unable to say a word. He only heard the general's warm and friendly voice and felt his father's good strong hand on his shoulder. He did not know that but a few hours before, Antonio Sousa, tense and worried, had rushed to see General Zeilin, and implored him to take his boy into the band lest he run away with a circus. And the general, a father himself, had agreed to induct Philip that very morning. As an apprentice he would have to put up the music stands, distribute the parts, run all sorts of errands, and perfect his trombone playing so that he could, in due course, join that section. And, having been sworn in as a member of the United States Marines, the mere thought of wandering circuses would be tantamount to desertion.

Philip was the proudest boy in Washington. The Marine

Band was one of the two oldest bands in the country, nearly as old as West Point's. It had developed from a handful of drummers and fifers who had recruited volunteers for George Washington, and it had played for every President thereafter. It had played at every Inaugural Ball since Madison's; it had played for Polk during the Mexican War; it had been at Gettysburg, and at Lincoln's funeral; and it also played on festive occasions, like egg-rolling parties on the White House grounds.

Philip would wear the glorious red uniform with the blue pants and edges and trimmings of gold. He would march on parade in time with the leader, down Pennsylvania Avenue, right into the White House. None of his friends could boast of having been within the President's four walls. Maybe he would one day be first trombonist or drum major; maybe he would be President of the United States . . . there was no limit to the opportunities of one who had become a public servant at 13!

That evening, at home, he looked at his watch. Now the circus was preparing to depart. He had to laugh over his childish desire of the day before!

Enlistment papers gave his size as four feet, nine inches, and, oddly enough, his "trade or occupation" as cabinet-maker. John Philip Sousa, aged 13 years, six months, and three days, pledged himself to "bear true allegiance to the United States of America," to "serve them honestly and faithfully against all their enemies or opposers," and to observe and obey the orders of the President and appointed officers for a period of seven years, five months, and 27 days.

The men in the band treated him like a mascot. They helped with his chores and showed him short cuts. When they marched through the streets, Philip carried his handsome head very high on his long, thin neck, and very proudly. Envious neighborhood boys might snap to mock attention when he showed up, and Ed Accardi said something about the people who ran to the Marines for shelter because they were afraid of circus lions. Philip didn't care. He was moving in a different world, in a different generation.

The year 1869 became a decisive one, the most decisive perhaps in Sousa's adolescence. In this year he heard two concerts which would determine his entire approach to music.

One concert was that of five children who performed as "The Franko family"—three girls and two boys, aged seven to 14. They were dressed in brown velvet and each played both piano and violin. The children hailed from New Orleans but had been trained in Germany from where they had only recently returned for their first American concert in Steinway Hall. Sam, the older boy, aged 12, had already played the Mendelssohn concerto in Berlin, two years before; but Philip was even more impressed by Nahan, the youngest. "It was the first time I had heard real violin playing and the exquisite performance of little Nahan Franko, who was a wonder on the instrument, inspired me with zeal to do better," he reminisced more than half a century later. Yes, indeed; what a seven-year-old could do should give no trouble to John Philip Sousa, nearly 15.

The other concert was by the orchestra of Theodore Thomas who had just started his musical crusade that was to convert the inland cities into music centers within a matter of years. They came to Washington toward the end of their first tour that had led them as far west as Chicago. The program included Schumann's *Träumerei*, an ethereal piece of music, in Thomas' own arrangement for strings alone. Muted for the final portion, they produced a deeply exciting diminuendo, a pianissimo such as the audience had never heard before. And then Thomas had his violinists continue to draw their bows even after the piece had ended, leaving his listeners breathless, unable to distinguish when the music had really become inaudible. Such tricks, and others like hiding flutists in trees at outdoor concerts, were almost conservative as compared to extravagances that had to be invented at the time to make serious music palatable to novice audiences. Whatever the serious-minded Thomas may have thought of the necessity of catering to playful instincts, his arrangement of *Träumerei* was extremely effective and left Philip in a state of exaltation.

The concert kindled in him a powerful desire to write a piece of music no less sweet and enchanting. Next morning he took his violin and let the bow glide over the strings caressingly, and the string responded with a melody all his own. He played it over and over again, and each time he liked it better. He dashed into the living room and played it for his parents.

"Very nice," said Mother.

"Let me hear it once more," said Father and nodded gravely.

When neighbors came in later, Philip didn't need much urging to play it for them too. "Not quite as gay as *Dixie*," one said; and "Not quite as solemn as *Nearer My God to Thee*," said someone else; but they all found it pretty.

So that night before going to bed he sat down and wrote

it out, lovingly and neatly, complete with piano accompaniment. He even gave it a title, *An Album Leaf*, which he painted with clumsy, elaborate characters above the music. Next day he took it to his teacher.

Esputa was sitting at the piano when Philip entered. Without a word, yet with his heart beating a little faster, he put the music in front of the professor and raised the violin to his cheek. Esputa remained poker-faced as they played it through; then he took the sheet between scornful fingers, as if it were something disgusting, and tossed it away. "Cheese and bread, and bread and cheese," he said cryptically, in a tone indicating abysmal disdain. He said no more as Philip picked up his disgraced composition and took it home like an injured child.

Why had Esputa done this to him? Why didn't he at least tell him how to improve it? Why did he treat Philip's first humble attempt at putting his own notes together as if he had done something wrong? His first effort at musical creation had brought him his first deep grief.

He never again played it for anyone. He never had it published. But he often told its story, and when fans asked him what had become of it he would say that he had burned it. "The world does not stop to look at what it passed by," the great Sousa proclaimed. "It wants something new." But in his autobiography he claimed that it still constituted one of his most cherished treasures.

Yet the yellowed sheet with the youthful handwriting has not turned up in the papers he left behind.

chapter three

PHILIP now was certain that he wanted to be a violinist and a composer. He saw less and less of Esputa, and more and more of another teacher, Felix Benkert, a pianist-conductor of Georgetown, whom he always was to consider one of the greatest musicians of his day. Benkert was a quiet man with a brown beard, deep-set eyes, and a saint's features. Philip worshiped him. Lessons might last two, three hours, concentrating on harmony and composition. Then for relaxation teacher and pupil might play sonatas together—Haydn, Mozart, Beethoven. Philip also played first violin in Benkert's Orchestral Union, when off duty. His musical horizon widened steadily.

And as Benkert taught him to learn, Philip learned to teach. His first pupils were four Italian urchins, street fiddlers who came for violin lessons, leaving a smell of garlic all over the house; and a rich young man who wanted to learn to play *The Last Rose of Summer* on the cornet so that later on he might entertain his friends during yacht trips on the Potomac. Throughout the three months that he taught him, Philip could not interest him in another piece of music.

At that time he also made his debut as a conductor, with Mr. Kernan's vaudeville theater, an outdoor affair in a new summer garden where he conducted with violin and bow, like the Waltz King Johann Strauss. Rumors had it that Mr. Kernan, a former sailor, did not believe in the use of words to express discontent, and that some people had retained broken noses and shattered jaws as souvenirs of his disapproval. The very première had started with a rout: a downpour had flooded the garden so that the show had to be moved indoors. The piano was mutilated in the process, Philip's strings snapped one after another, the clarinetist got short of breath with tension, the drummer missed every cue, and the prima donna was near hysterics. When the thing was over, Kernan made for Philip like an avenging devil, but Philip made a sharp turn, Marine-style, and yelled at him about his hot, ramshackle theater and that he was resigning, until Kernan, who could not have found another conductor at that time of year, implored him to stay on. Philip felt it was not difficult to handle people; all you needed was common sense and a flair for dignity.

A waltz suite, *Moonlight on the Potomac*, ghost-written for an elderly swain who wanted to impress a very young girl, was the first composition for which Philip was paid. Some time before, he actually had to pay 25 dollars of his scant savings to a publisher to get a short piece of music printed, and even though all his friends bought copies, it never sold more than four dollars' worth.

He had been very unhappy over this venture. He failed to understand why the world, always looking for new tunes, was passing him by.

"You are too young," Benkert had tried to explain. "No one ever heard of you."

But after the *Moonlight* suite, Benkert did not object

when Philip announced that he was going to Philadelphia to see Lee & Walker, one of the leading publishers, about his new march, *The Review*, and *The Cuckoo*, a galop.

In Philadelphia Philip was ushered into the presence of Thomas à Becket, the editor. Philip liked him instantly, though he could hardly have foreseen that this tense moment would mark the beginning of a lifelong friendship.

"Do you want to play, or shall I?" à Becket asked.

"I'm not a very good pianist," Philip said gratefully.

After he was through, the editor murmured a few words which Philip didn't quite catch but which sounded friendly enough. Then, taking him down one flight of stairs to the office of Mr. Lee, he played the two pieces again.

"Very nice," Mr. Lee said slowly. "How old are you, Mr. Sousa? Eighteen . . . well . . ." A pause. "This is a difficult proposition . . . it's a gamble . . . might be a hit, might be a flop . . . we never know . . . and there's nothing the publisher can do . . . yet, your pieces are nice . . . we'd like to print them . . . if only your name were known . . ."

If my name were known, Philip thought, I wouldn't be standing here. I'd send him my manuscripts with my terms. (He was getting angry.) I've gambled already . . . train fare and hotel . . . 15 dollars, hard-earned cash . . . But, "To be known, my name has to appear in print," was all he said.

"Yes, yes," said Mr. Lee. "We might do something about this, son."

And while Philip was on tenterhooks, Lee looked at the ceiling as if waiting for inspiration. "We might print your two pieces and let you have one hundred copies of each."

"That's very nice," Philip said, "and how much money?"

"As I said, young man: one hundred copies of each piece. That costs money . . . we couldn't spend cash in addition."

Philip had no choice. At least, he didn't have to *pay* for the printing. He was making progress, step by step.

He expected immediate publication. But it took seven months and a dozen urgent letters, and finally he learned that his pieces would come out later in the year. Neither one ever became a hit.

Philip's social contacts had now completely shifted to the swanky Northwest. He cut a handsome figure in those surroundings: well mannered and well groomed, with his fine features and dense black hair and the drooping mustache he sported as soon as it would grow. He became one of the most popular young musicians in town, always ready to bring his violin for a benefit or amateur performance or a musical. His new friends also had intellectual ambitions. They had formed a literary club, the *Vis-à-Vis*, and published a little magazine containing their own poems and essays. Here Sousa made his debut as the prolific author who would, in the course of years, enrich literature by several books and innumerable articles. The young people met at regular intervals to discuss poetry, music, and paintings, and to read and perform their own works.

One day a girl read a poem, a sad poem, "The Song of the Sea." It struck a chord in Philip; a melody formed itself around the lines as she read. He asked her if she would allow him to set it to music. She blushed and gave him the sheet on which it was written. She had dreamy eyes, soft curls, and irresistible dimples when she smiled. Her name was Emma M. Swallow, and her father was a clergyman.

The Reverend Dr. Swallow was a big man with a booming voice. His wife seemed friendly and self-effacing. Both liked music. Emma had a sudden spurt of poetic inspiration and Philip's thoughts floated on tender melo, dies. But she was a stubborn girl and they had frequent tiffs. He was never quite sure about her feelings.

One day they quarreled so badly that he did not see her for several days. But then he received a poem by mail; "Ah Me!" Emma had called it, and it told the story of a brave knight who had left his beloved.

"And love is fleeting, love will go, no hand can stay its ebb and flow, and death is sweet when love has fled . . ." Philip read, and he rushed out, bareheaded, right to her house, and proposed.

She accepted.

But she insisted that her parents mustn't know.

This was hard for Philip to understand. He would have wanted to shout his happiness from the rooftops. He saw no reason to hide their engagement. It was dishonest toward their parents, humiliating for him and for her.

Was it, perhaps, his rather undistinguished position with the Marines? He was getting tired of it himself.

The novelty had long worn off. What remained was Monday morning inspection and the daily routine of distributing music sheets, of running errands, of practicing the trombone on the slim chance of being detailed to play. He was bored. And boredom was the last thing John Philip Sousa was able to endure, ever.

His term of enlistment would be over in December,

1875. He would be 21; rather overaged for an apprentice.

His father managed to get him re-enlisted, on July 8, 1872, to serve five years as a Principal Musician, Third Class, now five feet, six and three-quarter inches tall. But he did not enjoy his new status either.

His superiors must have realized that Philip was unhappy. Pay being small and careers slow, they saw no reason to keep the versatile young musician from spreading his wings. They granted lavish leaves of absence for outside work, and at a change in leadership they assigned him to write a march to greet the new man. This was a very unusual honor for the youngest Principal Musician in the band. Philip did his very best.

And yet, this very assignment brought things to a head.

The new leader was Louis Schneider, known for his unusual prowess on the clarinet. They assembled on the parade ground, as was customary on such occasions; and as Schneider and an aide appeared in the distance, the assistant leader gave the downbeat and the band struck up young Sousa's *Salutation March*. Philip had temporarily forgotten all his grievances. His cheeks were flushed, his eyes shone, and he blew into his trombone as powerfully as he knew how.

They finished just as Mr. Schneider reached the conductor's stand. He greeted the band formally, then asked what they had been playing.

"A new march by this boy over there," said the assistant leader, pointing at Philip, who stood tense with pride.

"Take it off the stands!"

The men were visibly embarrassed. Philip swallowed hard. This was more than he could take. This was unfair. An outright insult!

He could make a living as a musician anywhere. To him the Marine Band was just bread with very little butter. He would quit. The handsome uniform of which he had been so proud began to choke him like a strait jacket of humiliation.

But this was the Marines and one couldn't just quit. He had taken an oath. And desertion was punishable by "shooting at sunrise" . . .

Mr. Hunter was the only man who could help, the Honorable William Hunter, Under Secretary of State. Philip had been introduced to him by Dr. Swallow, and Mr. Hunter had taken a fancy to the young man. Every Tuesday night for about two years Philip played chamber music at the Hunter mansion, the only professional among distinguished amateurs, and his host never failed to slip a five-dollar bill into his pocket.

Sousa always credited Mr. Hunter for having first guided him on the road to serious study of musical history. Mr. Hunter would advertise in European periodicals for rare works unobtainable in the United States, and when one of the bulky packages of music arrived, he and Philip would study the scores together. Then Mr. Hunter would go over his vast library and read to Philip from foreign encyclopedias, translating as he read, about the strange and often-so-troubled lives of music's greats.

Philip was sure that Mr. Hunter would understand his predicament and use his influence to obtain an honorable discharge for him. Mr. Hunter himself had felt for some time that military routine had outlived its usefulness for Philip. Young Sousa needed a new challenge right now, chores more difficult and more rewarding. He promised to talk it over with Secretary of the Navy George M. Robeson, and the Secretary was amenable.

"You should go to Europe and complete your musical education," was Mr. Hunter's reaction when a grateful Philip displayed his discharge papers.

Philip said that his father couldn't possibly afford to send him abroad.

"I know a gentleman who would send you," Hunter suggested.

"I wouldn't want anybody to support me," Philip said proudly.

"I wouldn't be so particular about that. If the man wants to spend money to educate talented young musicians, why not let him do it?" And he made an appointment for Philip to see Mr. W. W. Corcoran, the noted philanthropist.

Still, Philip had misgivings. He didn't want to be anybody's protégé. And to him there could be no better teacher than Benkert.

He was unusually timid when he pulled Mr. Corcoran's bell. A butler opened the door. He looked awe-inspiring, a towering man in dark livery with white gloves and unfriendly eyes. His manner was superior when he listened to the boy's request and relaxed only slightly when Philip mentioned Mr. Hunter's name.

After a while Mr. Corcoran came downstairs, a friendly man who had made a vast fortune as a financier and spent a small fortune on his hobby: supporting artists and the arts. His manner was encouraging as he inquired about Philip's ultimate ambitions and listened with genuine interest.

Philip never quite remembered what he said to Mr.

Corcoran. He only remembered that, balancing on the edge of an antique chair, he was chilled by the stiff splendor of the surroundings, deadly frightened by the idea of owing anything to anyone.

"I'll think it over, and you call again in five or six days," Philip finally heard Mr. Corcoran say.

He jumped to his feet, thanked the old gentleman, promised to return, and knew that he would never see Mr. Corcoran again, that he would not return, not in five days or weeks or years, even though he might never see Europe. Swiftly he walked past the stiffening butler, ran downstairs, ran home.

chapter four

PHILIP never regretted his decision of renouncing the security of a federal position while, at the same time, refusing private sponsorship. He was never without work, never without pupils, and every new assignment meant, if not a promotion, at least an expansion of his activities, a new experience.

He immediately found a job as a violinist at Ford's Opera House while continuing his studies with Benkert, who also would advise him on the fingering of tricky passages in the music he played at the theater. First they performed Offenbach operettas. Then one Milton Nobles moved in, a man whose handsome features were all but hidden by an enormous mustache and who wrote, produced, and acted in highly successful topical comedies. When Nobles came to Washington he had just scored a hit at Philadelphia's Colonel Wood's Museum with a play called *The Phoenix*, a dramatization of a newspaper story and a satire on the absurd language often used by journalists. His line, "And the villain still pursued her," became a catchword; wherever he went, local columns plugged the phrase.

Another of Nobles' plays, *Bohemians and Detectives*, gave Sousa his first big chance, when called upon, at a minute's notice, to replace the conductor who had fallen ill. Philip seized the baton with eagerness, ambition, determination. Conducting gave him a feeling of responsibility and achievement.

He conducted the simple incidental music as if it were a classic. He did not miss one cue and was pleased with conductor Sousa. So, evidently, was Milton Nobles. For a few days later, after his company had moved on, Nobles wired, asking whether Mr. Sousa would care to join him on the road as musical director.

The telegram came from Chicago. Philip had never as yet communicated with anyone so far away. And he had never as yet had such an offer . . .

The Middle West—this sounded intriguing. Philip had never been further than Philadelphia, except the one trip

33

to Boston with Father, years ago, which he remembered chiefly because he had stayed at a hotel for the first time and had had pie for breakfast. Now he had a chance to see, to learn—and quite on his own merits, no sponsor sending him.

Musical directorship at this time often included the composition of incidental music. He would write songs and dances for the cast, entrance and exit marches for the audience.

Normally he would have jumped at the chance. But there was Emma. He was no longer a free man. Thank God for that!

He could suggest that they get married, but could he take a clergyman's daughter on the road with a touring operetta? On the other hand, could he ask her to wait?

And because he didn't know how to tell her, he stalled. One day, two days.

On the third day, when he went to see her, the maid led him into her father's study. Dr. Swallow seemed a changed man, and not a friendly one. His powerful eyes stared at Philip icily, and then his voice, trained in a lifetime of public oratory, roared, "Young man, you have come to my house like a thief in the night and stolen my daughter!"

"Stolen?" Philip gasped.

"What right have you to become engaged to my daugter?"

So Emma had talked, at long last. "Well, she had to become engaged to *someone*," he said sheepishly.

The minister chose to ignore the impropriety. "This engagement must end!" he thundered.

"Why?" Philip seemed to grow a few inches taller. "Do you object to me as a man?"

"No."

"To my family . . . ?"

"I object to you because you are a musician."

"There is no nobler profession in the world!"

For a moment Dr. Swallow was startled by the tone of passionate conviction. He grew a shade friendlier.

"I am willing to grant that, but point out to me, if you can, one musician who ever had a dollar. . . . My daughter has been brought up with every luxury. . . ."

Philip reached into the pocket in which he carried Mr. Nobles' telegram. But he changed his mind. No use now.

Instead, he declared stoutly that he would leave town at once. He would not communicate with Emma for two years. If he didn't succeed financially within that period of time, he would give her up. But if he did succeed, and if she still loved him, he would marry her.

"I'll never consent!" Dr. Swallow shouted.

"And I don't care! Good day!"

Philip stalked out of the house.

Two days later, he joined Mr. Nobles and the company at Streator, Illinois.

He did not permit himself to be miserable.

chapter five

AMERICA was musically young. In the big cities
concert life had flourished for several decades, but in the hinterland the pioneers still
went on building. As the Wild West was settling, music
moved in from the East.

First, Theodore Thomas and his 54-piece orchestra
blazed the trail for classical music, and even for Wagner,
at a time when the "music of the future" was the most
controversial issue, the favorite scandal, in the musical
world abroad. Then Patrick Gilmore, the master showman,
plastered with medals and diamond buttons, started out
West, introducing Beethoven and Schubert arranged for
band.

In Gilmore's wake, and all along the "Thomas High-
way," which reached from New England to the Pacific
coast, small orchestras and bands sprouted, formed by
people who had first come to listen, on horseback and in
wagons, from many hours away. When Philip started touring, the big cities were still provincial, the small ones had a
newness about them; but even the smallest had an "opery
house," fitted out with the latest comforts and equipment
of the 1870's.

Streator, Illinois, wasn't even a town. It had been incor-
porated as a village only a few years before, when its popu-

lation had been less than 1500. But people predicted that the coal mines right under the fertile rolling prairie country would make Streator the Pittsburgh of the West.

When Philip arrived, Mr. Nobles sent him at once to find a small orchestra, call a rehearsal, and have it ready for a performance that night.

Philip had never held an audition, had never hired musicians, except for his little dance band years ago; and he hadn't handled *that* too smartly, he now remembered. He felt a little lost as he walked through Main Street in search of orchestra players.

At the theater he was told that the musicians' representative might be located in a paint shop nearby.

He found his man all stained and sweating, puffing on a big cigar, weighing cement on a huge scale. Yes, he could supply any number of musicians, he growled, at two dollars a skull.

Philip wanted five strings, four wind players, and a drum, and demanded that all ten skulls report for rehearsal at 2 P.M. sharp.

The man drew himself up full length: "Stranger, there are just two things that you don't want here. One is that you don't want any first fid, and you don't want any viola or celly and you don't want no flute, 'cause we ain't got 'em. The second thing you don't want is a rehearsal at two o'clock or any other time."

"But," Philip said, "we *must* have a rehearsal!"

"We never rehearse here!"

"But my music is difficult! Can your orchestra transpose?"

"We transpose anything."

37

And since this was the only orchestra in Streator, it was a take-it-or-leave-it proposition.

At 7 P.M. Philip found the musicians in a room under the stage.

"You might just as well know the boys," the man from the paint shop greeted him. "What is your name?"

"Sousa."

"Well, Sousa, allow me to introduce Professor Smith, our second fid; and, Sousa, this is Professor Brown, our clarinet player; and, Sousa, this is Professor Perkins"; and then there were Professor Jones, two Professors Simpson, Professor Reed. Philip then explained that they were using an overture he had written for Mr. Nobles, and would the professors, please, skim it through. "It has been well received," he added.

"It won't go here," the paint shop man decreed. "Will it, boys?"

"No!" it came back in unison.

"But . . . my overture is all right . . ."

"It may be all right in Chicago or Bosting, but it won't go here. I got the overture that our people want and that's the one we're going to play . . . Do you read first fid at sight?"

The audience was already arriving. Philip had no choice.

"When you are playin' that first strain," the man briefed him, "you do it just as if you didn't have no train to ketch, but here," he pointed at the allegro, "you'll have to chase your fingers all over the fiddle."

The musicians were hopelessly inadequate. When they came to the allegro, they hobbled after Philip, each man as fast as he could. As Philip struggled through the chaos, stamping and beating time with his violin, he had the vision of a horse race—the field wide apart; and when the first crossed the finishing line, the last straggler was several bars behind. After the overture the curtain rose on a vocal number; now they didn't only play in different time but also in different keys.

"E flat!" Philip shouted. The men played louder so the audience wouldn't hear him.

"E flat!!!" Philip roared. Ten instruments, completely off pitch, drowned him out. A forlorn singer struggled bravely to be heard over the cacophony in the pit. After the number was over, an irate Philip swore that he had never, never before, heard such a rotten orchestra.

"If you don't like our style of playin', pay us and we'll go," the paint shop man said casually.

"You haven't earned a cent! Get out!"

"When we are paid!"

And while Mr. Nobles' persevering performers kept the show going, the musical director rushed out and buttonholed the manager and the theater superintendent.

"All right," the latter said, "just call the constable and put them out as usual."

And as the policeman proceeded to get the orchestra out, Philip said to the local manager, "And when I wanted them to come to a rehearsal they said they never rehearsed in this town."

"That's true . . . if they did they would be discharged before the performance."

And so the music which Sousa had written for Milton Nobles' play *The Phoenix*, never got a hearing in Streator, Illinois.

Philip got used to trouble as they traveled on,

39

through Kansas and Nebraska and Alabama, playing in large cities and small. In one town an actor fell into an open fire trap; in another the theater burned down the night before their performance. In Kansas the city band offered to get the town out by playing in front of the theater, gratis, if they could see the show afterward, with their instruments serving as passes. This seemed a fair proposition, judging by the masses of townspeople who came to listen to the band. But Philip could hardly have foreseen that the musicians, once inside, would pass their instruments through ground-floor windows to friends waiting in the street, who, in turn, passed them to others, so that at least a hundred "band musicians" had gone in before Philip had the windows locked.

In Mobile, Alabama, he found a fairly good orchestra with an old German leader. The man attached himself to Philip's coattails, showered him with compliments, shared his every meal, and finally asked him to accept the dedication of a small piece of music he had just written to immortalize their friendship. He conducted it for Philip one morning during rehearsal, a pretty polka which he promised to send on to New Orleans, the Nobles company's next stop.

Philip was amazed when the New Orleans concertmaster asked him slyly whether, by any chance, a piece of music had been dedicated to him at Mobile. The old gentleman, it turned out, was pulling the trick on every conductor who passed through town. The manuscript, the concertmaster estimated, had been the leader's meal ticket for at least half his lifetime, which certainly was more than Beethoven could say for any of his symphonies.

Philip, of course, never received his copy.

chapter six

THE two-year probation period was not even half over when Nobles' tour came to an end. Philip returned to Washington. It was good to be home and back at his old job at Ford's. It almost seemed as if everybody had been waiting for his return. Philip avoided the *Vis-à-Vis*, and he avoided Emma; not to see her hurt more than he had thought.

His duties with the theater varied, according to the company that rented it. He fiddled or conducted. He wrote some incidental music. Early in 1876 he left again on tour.

His new employer was Matt Morgan who had done art work for *Leslie's Weekly* and now traveled with a series of "Living Pictures" on mythological and antique subjects, posed by seven ravishingly pretty girls and one lone male. The shocking novelty drew auditoriumfuls of gay stag parties all along the road; but in Pittsburgh morals-conscious authorities put the girls in jail. The trial next morning was a burlesque show in itself. Morgan hired the best lawyer in town, who first delivered a learned address on art in the nude, then showed the officer a picture of a statue of Minerva, asking him whether he had ever arrested that woman.

"I arrest so many people, I can't remember all of them," the policeman snapped. The case was dismissed. But Philip had enough.

He was so thoroughly fed up, in fact, that he left Matt Morgan halfway en route to the Pacific coast and returned East, to Philadelphia, where the Centennial Festival was in progress, the largest exposition America had as yet seen.

The United States was celebrating its 100th birthday by displaying the latest industrial achievements from all over the world. The "International Exhibition of Arts, Manufacture, and Products of the Soil and Mine," was held on a 450-acre plot of Fairmount Park, which the city of Philadelphia had transferred to the Centennial Committee in a Fourth of July ceremony three years before. A town of 180 buildings had sprung up on the grounds, huge halls, parks, restaurants, which were to admit 9,500,000 people in the course of six months.

Theodore Thomas was musical director; and he had commissioned music for the opening ceremony from America's leading composers, John K. Paine and Dudley Buck, as well as from his great favorite across the ocean: a 5000-dollar fee had persuaded Richard Wagner to take time out from rehearsals for the first Bayreuth Festival to compose the *Centennial Inaugural March* to the strains of which President Grant would make his appearance. Four years before, Gilmore had imported Johann Strauss for his monumental *Boston Peace Jubilee*, paying the Waltz King 100,000 dollars to compensate him for his agonizing fear of travel accidents. Now, the Philadelphia committee engaged Strauss' French counterpart, Jacques Offenbach, whose satirical and slightly morbid operettas had made him music's *enfant terrible par excellence*.

Philip had been warned that he would starve in this town swarming with musicians scrambling for work, but he was almost at once engaged by Offenbach as a first violinist—a lucrative and entertaining job. Offenbach was a frail man with whiskers, a monocle, sparkling wit, and unlimited vanity. Sporting a dress coat, black trousers, white cravat, and gray gloves, he conducted his naughty tunes with grace and dignity. In his programs he showed considerable bias for his own compositions, one of the few exceptions being *The International Congress* by first violinist John Philip Sousa, which started with a fugue on *Yankee Doodle*, swept through the national anthems of practically the entire world, and closed with the *Star-Spangled Banner*, treated in parodistic imitation of the *Tannhäuser* overture. Offenbach encouraged anything that helped to deflate Wagner who a few years ago, when Paris was besieged by the Germans, had ridiculed him in a satirical poem.

Offenbach's was the largest orchestra in which Philip had ever played. Its 75 members sat on a podium in the center of a supersized winter garden, surrounded by tropical plants, grass plots, shrubs, and flower beds, between which people promenaded when there was room to move. Boxes looking like Swiss cottages were in the corners, and there was a large gallery with more boxes and tiers. Multicolored lampions hung from the ceiling, their odd light effects artfully broken by huge mirrors and crystals. A miniature Niagara Falls opposite the entrance sent down roaring cascades of water during intermissions. The whole thing was called Offenbach Garden and was at the corner of Broad and Cherry streets.

Thomas' new Music Hall was even more elaborate. But America's favorite conductor was out of luck. Wagner's march had turned out to be a thoughtless, commonplace composition which Thomas himself considered an unforgivable insult; and the public didn't like the stuffy atmosphere of the auditorium in which no refreshments were sold. And while the conductor's heavy figure labored through heavy scores and the heat of a Philadelphia summer, "with little spirit," as Offenbach remarked, "looking from behind like a bird vainly trying to take to the air," Offenbach Garden was so overcrowded that an ingenious manager decided to by-pass the closing regulation that prevailed on Sundays. To Offenbach, who was considered so objectionable in Paris that the censor had limited him to skits with only three characters, it sounded like one of his own jokes when he learned that he, of all people, was to conduct a Grand Sacred Concert on Sunday morning, in the City of Brotherly Love. But the manager, who had advertised the event for a full week, was keenly disappointed when the authorities withdrew permission at the last minute. Evidently their notions about programs of sacred music differed from their distinguished guest's, who had included, besides selections from Schubert and Gounod, the Litanie from his *La Belle Hélène*, a Hymn from *Orpheus in the Underworld*, a Prayer from *La Grande Duchesse de Gerolstein*, and a burlesque polka which he thought might pass for sacred because its title was *Seraphic Dance*.

Then, on July 4, Patrick Gilmore started his two-month engagement with a mammoth concert in Independence Square. To Philip, who had never heard Gilmore, this was the greatest event of all. He hadn't thought much about band music during those years in theater pits, but his hearing Gilmore struck the old, passionate chord. Yes, a band was the answer to a musician's prayer. Gilmore was right: a band was virile and heroic; symphony orchestras were effeminate in comparison. Before Gilmore, bands had only been for parades. He was the first to visualize an indoor band for concert purposes, in which woodwinds would take over for the strings; and in 1873 he had assembled 100 ace players, every one of them well worth the fabulous salaries which were as high as 750 dollars a week.

When Johnny comes marching home, the band played, the tune that Gilmore claimed as his own—and all of a sudden Philip was the little boy again, who stood on a wooden platform on Pennsylvania Avenue and saw the soldiers march by. Eleven years had passed since—and again the sky was blue, and the banners waved—and it was the same music . . .

"Music will never die," he exulted. "Doesn't the Bible say that Gabriel will wake us all on Judgment Day with a trumpet . . . ?"

After Offenbach left, Philip didn't know what to do. He could have returned to Washington; he might have tried New York. Then the problem solved itself: Simon Hassler, conductor at the Chestnut Street Theater, offered him a job in the orchestra.

So there he was again, sitting in a pit, except that this company had a larger and better orchestra than even Ford's, and an extremely fine roster of actors. Philip also played part time in another orchestra; he gave lessons; he corrected proofs; he wrote incidental music for Hassler, a number of small pieces for his publisher, and an elaborate *Te Deum*—for his shelves. He also began to look for a librettist, for he wanted to write an opera. He was busy and fairly satisfied.

The picture of Emma had begun to fade, when, walking

45

down Chestnut Street one day, he ran into her with her father. Dr. Swallow was very friendly; Emma had hardly changed. The two years were over. He had made no riches, but he was not ashamed of his record either. No harm in showing off a bit, he said to himself as he invited the Swallows for dinner at a hotel slightly on the expensive side—but not too much so. He talked a lot and asked few questions. He elaborated on his activities as a teacher, composer, editor, violinist; he told witty stories, and he was again very much in love.

The party cost him half a week's budget, but it seemed a sound investment. Two days later he had a note from Emma, a week-end invitation.

He felt happy and relaxed during his long talk with Dr. Swallow on Sunday after dinner. Everything had become so simple, he thought as he waited for Emma to get dressed for a walk. But then Mrs. Swallow entered, all kindness and sweetness. She put her hand on his shoulder and smiled at him fondly. "Philip, dear boy, I'm worried," she said.

"Why?"

"Em may love you, but . . . there is a man much older than she, a splendid man, an officer in the Confederate Army . . . he loves her dearly. . . . Of course, she will marry you if you insist . . . but are you sure you will be happy?"

"I . . . understand . . ." Philip was too stunned to say more. He made a move to rid himself of that hand on his shoulder that now seemed to burn him. She pressed his fingers lightly and slipped away like a mischievous mouse.

Young as he was, Sousa had developed a faculty of looking a situation squarely in the eye. No fuss, no if's, no but's.

46

No fretting afterward. Once he had come to a decision, he stuck to it and dismissed the whole thing from his mind.

He could take his walk with Emma and quiz her about the elderly officer. He could try to find out more diplomatically whether her mother had any special plans for her and wanted to discourage their match. He could even say nothing, wait to see if Emma had anything to tell him, and if she didn't then he could disregard the whole affair. He felt inclined to do just that as he paced the living room, pondering.

Yet, ". . . if you insist . . ." it lingered in his ears. He didn't want to be married for old times' sake, with a regretful thought of someone else . . . of some has-been in uniform—an old man—a former rebel—how *could* she!? And quite explosively it occurred to him that he didn't really know this girl . . . maybe she was a coquette, just toying around . . . now he remembered how she had temporized when they first talked marriage, hadn't wanted to announce their engagement . . .

"Here I am!" Emma entered, pretty and all radiant smiles.

Philip grabbed his hat and coat. "I'm going."

"Where?"

"To Philadelphia, on the four o'clock train."

"But why?" she was startled.

"Ask—your—mother!" It sounded like three stones hurled with a hard hand.

The front door snapped shut.

Monday he had a letter from her, asking him not to be foolish. He didn't answer; he *didn't* want to be a fool. Wednesday an ultimatum reached him from Washington: unless his immediate reply would be forthcoming, she

47

would marry the other man. One week later he received a marked copy of the Washington *Evening Star*, announcing the betrothal of Miss Emma M. Swallow.

chapter seven

O N MAY 25, 1878, Gilbert and Sullivan's *H. M. S. Pinafore* had its première at London's Opéra Comique. Due to an unprecedented heat wave of 70 degrees and topical jokes that Queen Victoria's subjects didn't particularly enjoy, the good ship floundered haplessly through listless waters and might have gone on the rocks had not America come to its rescue. *Pinafore* was six months old to the day when Montgomery Field—despite gloomy warnings that Gilbert and Sullivan would never go over with Americans—imported it to the Boston Museum, where it scored an instant hit which reverberated across the ocean and filled the London theater as well. It was the impact of the American success that merged Gilbert and Sullivan into the famous team, the most discordant pair that ever worked together, constantly at odds and yet indispensable to each other to the very end.

Pinafore provided precisely the kind of entertainment Americans had missed. They weren't sensitive about Gilbert's disrespect for "the Queen's Navee"; his fun was clean and clever, "innocent but not imbecile," as he said. Now even dowagers and young girls could go to a show without running the danger of seeing other females in tights and corsets, singing ambiguous lines translated from the French. Gilbert's snappy lyrics which made him *persona non grata* at the Court of St. James made musical comedy respectable in the United States.

A mass craze broke loose, unprecedented in theatrical history. About a hundred companies gave the opera—amateurs and professionals, church choirs and school groups. *Pinafore* was performed as a drama, comedy, burlesque. One hundred thousand barrel organs ground out *Pinafore*. Americans spoke in *Pinafore* quotations, played *Pinafore* games, ate, drank, breathed, swam in, whistled *Pinafore*.

In Philadelphia Mr. Childs, editor of the *Public Ledger* and a gentleman of tremendous consequence, took himself to the show and wrote an editorial about its purity. Now even the most prudish members of society who had never been to a theater were won over.

The *Pinafore* whirl eventually seized also Philip, when Thomas à Becket recommended him as a coach, to prepare the opera with Mrs. Keene's singing class. Mrs. Keene was the voice teacher *en vogue*, society's fad. Whoever wanted to belong to the smart set enrolled daughter or son with Mrs. Keene. And for Mrs. Keene *Pinafore* was a god-

49

send; it was increasingly difficult to find light operas which were both proper and easy to sing.

So for a generous 10 dollars a night Philip coached what he considered the finest assembly of voices and beauties he had ever met. And just because they were so charming and distinguished, he was extremely difficult at rehearsals. He later claimed to have produced the best singing cast among the many *Pinafore* companies.

The Philadelphia Church Choir Company, as the hopefuls called their group to attract the last-ditch recalcitrants, even went on the road. Chaperoned by Mrs. Keene, they played in Wilmington, Trenton, Pottsville, and other towns close enough for them to return the same night.

February 22, 1879, was to be the most memorable day in Philip's life.

The birthday chorus greeted him as he entered the theater, and on the table were glasses filled with something that was supposed to pass for punch.

"Celebrating George Washington?" he asked.

"I'd like you to meet Jane van Middlesworth Bellis, Professor," one of the girls said. "Jennie, time you met the boss."

Philip saw a cloud of chestnut hair under a gray bonnet, delicate features with a sweet smile, and a peach complexion. The girl wasn't tall but very graceful, and charmingly dressed. She sang in the chorus, he now vaguely remembered, but they had never been introduced.

"There are two birthdays today," she twittered as they shook hands. "Washington's and . . ."

"And whose . . . ?"

Mine. I'm sixteen . . .

Sixteen. Sixteen. Sweet sixteen.

50

On his own sixteenth birthday Father, with a wide the-atrical gesture, had offered him his first cigar. He had been sick for the rest of the day.

It was good to have a family. He was longing for them. Since his rift with Emma he had been working hard, bury-ing himself in work as a means of escape. That's why he had written so many sentimental songs, songs which had comprised the bulk of his compositions during the past year or so. He was lonely.

Two weeks later the company went to New York. A pro-fessional manager took over the Philadelphia Church Choir Company or, rather, retained the name and kept Sousa on. Their new *Pinafore* production opened at the Broadway Theater on March 10. An old company was still running at another theater, a third one opened the same day, a still fourth one would have its première soon. There were plenty of audiences in New York for anyone who wanted to give *Pinafore*, and plenty of opportunities for a handsome young musician to have a good time.

Philip didn't have a good time, however. He was moon-ing. For the first time he was in revolt against a fate and a profession which tossed him about, like a straw in the wind, at the mercy of the fad of the moment. He promenaded on Fifth Avenue. Girls fluttered by and left him cold. He looked at his cast, scrutinized it carefully—and noticed with pleasure that none of the girls was as pretty as a certain girl in Philadelphia. He took to the habit of checking the audiences; March went by, April was nearly over, and still, to his secret delight, he had not seen one single woman who had Jane's delicate beauty and well-mannered poise.

After seven weeks the show closed. They had a return engagement for May, but there was a fortnight of grace.

He hurried to Philadelphia. Jane blushed and her fingers trembled slightly as they lay in his. Life was beautiful . . .

Theirs was no stormy, exciting courtship. No obstacles were put in their way. No Victorian father or overambitious mother found that Philip wasn't good enough. Mr. Bellis, one of the most distinguished citizens of Philadelphia, was a short, fair-haired gentleman with engaging manners.

"But she still goes to school," he remonstrated mildly. "And she can't cook . . ."

"She won't have to." Philip's breast inflated. "I shall hire a cook for her!" He then had 150 dollars to his name, and no steady income in sight.

Mr. Bellis may have had an inkling of this state of affairs, but he sensed in Philip personality, courage, initiative.

There was still a summer of *Pinafore* to endure, and in the fall a short-lived experiment with Sullivan's earlier *The Contrabandist.*

In December Philip was back in Philadelphia. On New Year's Eve he was a married man, and composer of a song, *When you change your name to mine . . .*

chapter eight

T HERE was something wrong with the Marine Band. Lieutenant Colonel McCawley thought so, and so did Commandant Zeilin. The band played listlessly, there were constant squabbles, and now serious charges had been brought against Louis Schneider. The investigating board of officers recommended instant discharge, and on October 1, 1880, the "President's own band" would be leaderless.

There were only two weeks left.

"I heard an operetta last time I was in Philadelphia," McCawley said to Zeilin. "Young Sousa conducted . . . gifted young man . . . efficient job. . . . Isn't his father still in the band?"

"He resigned last year," Zeilin said. "He's right over at my house, repairing furniture."

"Hm . . ." It was quite obvious what the colonel was thinking.

Zeilin's thoughts wandered in the same direction. He went straight home where he found Antonio Sousa busy with one of his chairs.

Philip, the proud father reported, was on tour with his own operetta, *Our Flirtations*. He had written it last summer, while vacationing with his bride at Cape May. It had taken him only a few weeks—he could do anything—his fantasy on *Carmen* was a masterpiece, to name only one. Anyhow, the show had been so successful in Philadelphia that Philip had taken it on the road; a good chance to show Jane a bit of country.

Zeilin listened, nodded, expressed his pleasure about all this good news, went back to McCawley, then back to Antonio Sousa, and Antonio said he would write his son.

The letter was waiting for Philip at their St. Louis hotel.

Jane, who was doing the unpacking, heard her husband whistle, which was a most unusual thing for him to do, and turned around. He handed her the letter.

Quickly she scanned the opening sentence. Father said that they should come to Washington at once; the post of Marine Band leader was waiting for Philip. She thought that this was very remarkable indeed; but for Philip it was supreme triumph, glorious vindication for his only setback so far.

It required a momentous decision, however. It meant giving up a colorful, varied career which he was just beginning to enjoy. It meant a life of military discipline, and he was not quite sure how he would like that. On the other hand, a salary of 1500 dollars a year was pretty good for a young couple, and the assignment carried much prestige.

He would be the youngest leader the Marine Band had ever had, and the first native Washingtonian. And it would be a noble task. He knew what was needed to make the band the best in the country. New blood was needed, youth, individual initiative, to meet the challenge of Gilmore and his imitators.

St. Louis seemed to be his city of destiny. He had left Matt Morgan's show in St. Louis, and if he hadn't done that he might never have met Jane.

He tried to imagine himself as the Marine Band leader, marching down Pennsylvania Avenue, beating time with that long white baton—trim, disciplined, wearing the splendid uniform, no less splendid but far more distinguished than anything Gilmore could think up. He loved uniforms, flags, decorations, the sound of feet marching to sprightly music. He would much rather write a genuine march than a manufactured symphony. He wanted to be a conductor, and he loved the sound of a band. It was in his blood.

He and Jane pondered for the rest of the day and, after they had gone to bed, through most of the night. But then, as the stars began to pale, a frightening question rose in Philip's mind: "But Pat, how do we know I can *do* the job?" (For some unexplained reason he always called her Pat.)

"If anyone can do it, *you* can." Her faith in him was touching. From their first day together to the very last, she was unshakably convinced that whatever he did he would do better than anyone else.

That settled it. "So all I've got to do is grow a beard to get some discipline out of those old buzzards," he muttered contentedly and rolled over.

Father waited at the station, radiating joy and pride. Antonio Sousa was mighty pleased with himself. How clever of him to have remained on good terms with everybody at the Marines! Hadn't he plugged Philip every time he had a chance, talked about his success as a conductor, his ability to get along with people, about every composition that had been published, about the distinguished family into which he had married? He had kept Philip in the news, or, at least, on the grapevine. Being a well-mannered man, he had never unduly boasted, never overdone, but he had certainly paved the way.

"The band gives me more trouble than all the rest of the corps put together," the commandant said when Philip reported for duty on October 1. Bandleader Sousa promised to investigate and submit suggestions.

He found the musicians overworked, underpaid, and grouchy. That they had no regular military status, yet couldn't get a discharge, irked them no end. Morale was at an all-time low. So was the repertory: some operatic selections, a few overtures, and, for the rest, marches and polkas of the crudest and most obvious kind; not one bar of those sensational contemporaries—Wagner, Berlioz, Tchaikovsky, Grieg—which the smallest amateur bands tried to play. The President's own band was no better than any of those that might play on village squares on Sundays; and at the weekly parade on the White House grounds the only people who stopped to listen were carriage-pushing nursemaids and bums.

The men were extremely poor, and quarrelsome as a result. With salaries ranging from 13 to 38 dollars a month and pathetically small allotments for food, fuel, and clothing, private engagements were their principal sources of income; and whenever official duties interfered with "outside business," trouble was bound to arise.

Sousa at once realized the fallacy of trying to get decent work out of people in this frame of mind. At least they should be free to leave. His first suggestion was that applications for release, if filed with his approval, be granted without delay. The commandant consented to try.

Next day a man put down his instrument and said that all this rehearsing was too much for him.

"What do you propose to do about it?" Philip challenged him.

"I want my discharge," the man said morosely.

Sousa was sorry to lose this particular man, but he wanted to establish a precedent as quickly as possible. "Make out your application and I'll get it for you," he said.

The man sneered. He didn't really mean to leave the band, and he was thoroughly shocked when he had his discharge 24 hours later.

Philip went to work on the repertoire. He made selections from the most recent European catalogues and held rehearsals more rigid than the men had ever known before. That some of them were older than his father didn't bother him in the least.

The band's first official function under Sousa was to play at the New Year's reception of outgoing President Hayes. They stood near the staircase between the East room and the reception room, where an endless stream of people came to shake hands with the President and the First Lady. As Philip prepared the music he remembered how uncomfortable President Grant and his guests had always been on such occasions, having to make careful and diplomatic conversation over the full blast of a military band. Even then he had wondered why the band wasn't toned down indoors. This was precisely what he was going to do. Some percussion players grumbled, but Sousa made it plain that those who didn't like it might apply for discharge.

The ambassadors arrived, then came the cabinet and the Supreme Court. Sousa, closely watching the President, molded the music to his every gesture and facial expression,

The music was soft, not in the least martial; the drums, tympani, cymbals, sounded as if covered with velvet. The President looked relaxed. When someone wanted to say something to him, he could understand without strain.

Arrivals grew in number, decreased in importance: officers stationed in Washington and departmental chiefs shook hands with the Chief Executive to the pleasant strains of operettas. And when the general public swarmed in, the Marine Band broke into marches, polkas, hornpipes, not noisy but in lively rhythms which accelerated everybody's step and got them dancing and prancing past the reception line. Afterward the President's secretary sought Philip out: "The President wants me to tell you that this was a splendid idea. He is much less exhausted than ordinarily after receptions, though he shook hands with twice the number of people."

"You've made it, Mr. Philip," said one of the older men in the band, who had known him since childhood, and touched his arm as they filed out.

chapter nine

AT THIS time the young Sousas lived with Philip's parents, at 502 Seventh Street, South East. The old frame cottage in which he had grown up had been converted into a brick house; Philip had done so well on the road that he had been able to send the money for the remodeling job.

Three younger brothers were still at home: George, Antonio, and Louis. Antonio was a postal clerk, with the family passion for sports and a flair for words, which eventually would turn him into one of the most popular sports writers in the country. George played the triangle and cymbals in the Marine Band. Philip gave him the additional duties of librarian; he needed a reliable and congenial person to take care of the growing stacks of new music. Every morning he and George left together, walking one and a half blocks to the "garrison," as the Marines called their barracks. Every mid-morning Father would put his tools or books away, throw his old Spanish cape over his shoulders, and follow his sons to watch a bit of rehearsal. When their father's peculiar, unmistakable silhouette turned up in the distance, Philip and George knew that they had another half-hour to go until lunch. Meantime Elizabeth Sousa prepared a rich meal, elaborate, German fashion; so Jane didn't have to do any cooking, after all.

In the afternoon Philip worked on his repertory, selecting and arranging music and, last not least, composing.
The young couple didn't have much space to themselves,
but one of the first pieces of furniture they acquired was a
high desk, such as bookkeepers used in their offices, so he
could either stand or sit. As long as he stayed in Washington, he composed practically all his marches, songs, and
operettas at this desk, while Jane perched on a stool beside
him, an assortment of quill pens in her lap, which she
handed to him, one by one. She could spend hours watching her husband, happy when her silent presence was
acknowledged by a furtive smile. They were young and
very much in love.

In 1881 their first child was born, John Philip, Jr. Later
that fall Jane had an attack of malaria. Veteran Washing-
tonians were used to it; in the marshland city, with sanitary
conditions still poor, it was the government officials' occu-
pational disease. But the delicate young mother was struck
with unusual violence. Spells of fever kept her listless,
apathetic. Then, again, in near-delirium, she had dreams
she couldn't remember except for the terror they had
caused her. In clearer moments she was agonized by the
thought of being unattractive to her husband. She asked
for her mirror. They didn't give it to her. But as soon as
she was better, she insisted.

She started up with a shock. "No . . ." she moaned and
sank back into her pillows.

"Philip likes it," she heard her mother-in-law say. "He
says it makes you even prettier."

Jane's hair had turned snow white.

Combined with her young, transparent complexion, the

60

white hair turned her into a ravishing beauty. And her children, John Philip, Jane Priscilla, and Helen, born within several years, never realized that their mother was growing older. Jane came to like her white hair. She would mix egg yolks into her shampoo, and gradually her coiffure, fluffy as a cloud, acquired a golden glimmer.

"Mother's halo," the children called it.

"My lovely blue-eyed bride," Sousa used to introduce his wife to strangers, and she never cared to remind him that her eyes were gray.

If Philip had feared that a regular life would be uneventful, he had been sorely mistaken. His adaptability and diplomatic skill were frequently challenged during the next 12 years which saw economic expansion under five different presidents; he had to be constantly on the alert for changes in personal tastes and policies. His quiet sense of humor often came in handy.

His service under President Garfield began and ended with an incident unique in White House history. The President chose to have the band summoned at one hour's notice, and Sousa's scouts managed to locate only one lone drummer. Orders being orders, however, Sousa and his man marched into the White House in full regalia and sat on the bandstand throughout the reception, after which Sousa dismissed the drummer with military ceremonial, and the two of them filed out.

This was his only White House appearance under Garfield, for not long after, on July 2, the President was shot at and seriously wounded by a political fanatic.

Sousa nearly had completed a hymn of thanksgiving for the recovery of the Chief Executive when one night in the fall he was aroused from sleep by newsboys shouting that the President had died. He got up and wandered aimlessly through Washington until the break of dawn. Then he sat down to write Garfield's Funeral March.

The Marine Band was stationed in front of the main stairway of the Capitol when the coffin was carried through the bronze door. The Marine Band also rode on the train that carried the body to Cleveland, and it led the funeral procession to the cemetery, playing Sousa's new march as they crossed through the gate. This was an impressive experience for a man not yet 27.

Chester L. Arthur, the new President, did not use the band during the period of national mourning, and, virtually free from official orders, Philip could drill his men as he saw fit. It suited him well that the rehearsal room was comparatively small. This taught him restraint and elimination; soft music is more difficult to produce than a sonorous tutti. Learning, he taught his men. He taught the band to whisper, to produce delicate orchestral effects. He taught it long, sustained tones that sounded like organ strains and brilliant virtuoso effects borrowed from the piano. "I fancy musicians still entertain a vague idea that a military band is inferior to the symphony orchestra; inferior it is not. It is simply different," he wrote some time later.

People began to comment on the improvement of the band. There was contrast in melody and rhythm, there were unusual harmonies, interesting, provocative—quite different from the monotonous blare of former years. In the summer the band played on Capitol Plaza Wednesdays, on the barrack grounds Thursdays, and on Saturday afternoons on the White House lawn.

It became fashionable to meet where the band played.

Women displayed their finery. Men talked business. Boys and girls stood hand in hand, swinging arms to the rhythm of the music. Carriages might stop for a few minutes. Sousa brought the Marine Band back into prominence. Until the rise of the automobile those outdoor concerts remained the most fashionable fair-weather pastime in the capital.

The band not only sounded rejuvenated; it also looked the part. Elderly grouchy men had been replaced by younger ones. On parades, right behind the young leader who sported gold-rimmed glasses and a dense black beard, came the trombones and basses, played by handsome youths who were able to march briskly and keep the regulation tempo of 120 beats a minute to the end. Not only urchins ran with the band; Philip, who had developed a faculty of seeing everything without moving his head, noticed distinguished-looking people escorting him, prominent businessmen, even members of Congress.

Never before had he accomplished so much with so little effort. Many an evening, when he changed from his uniform into the casual clothes he wore at home, he felt as if his working day had only started. He was not tired, but refreshed, receptive for musical inspiration. Also, he made new arrangements of practically everything the band played. He had decided to include as little as possible of the classical masters in his programs; the scores of Haydn, Mozart, Beethoven, were still based on string instruments, and band adaptations involved an amount of rescoring which he considered highhanded and unscrupulous. Romantic music, with its predominance of wind instruments, its emphasis on tone color and unusual detail, lent itself much better to the purpose.

His preoccupation with the serious music of his time led him toward sporadic attempts at elaborate composition. He had already written a "Historical Scene," *Sheridan's Ride*, and was contemplating a tone poem. Inevitably he was influenced by Liszt and Berlioz, but spiritually only, or rather, intellectually; for, even though he had all the novel orchestral effects at his command, his harmonies were simple and plain, not quite up to the musical sophistication of the day.

Bands all over the country were now playing his marches. Most of them were topical, written under the impression of an actual event or for a certain purpose. "I always need a stimulus from the outside to get musical inspiration," he said. *Across the Danube* commemorated the termination of another Russo-Turkish war, *The Yorktown Centennial* an important event in American history. *The Resumption* march owes its existence to the solution of a difficult domestic issue—the return to specie payment after a period of paper currency. *Guide Right, Guide Forward, The Wolverine*, as well as *Our Flirtation* (based on melodies from his operetta), won immediate popular acclaim.

And the lure of the human voice was as strong as ever. There were amateur writers galore in Washington, and literary clubs still flourished in exuberant self-confidence. Since, as was assumed, the most brilliant minds were required to govern God's own country, the assembly of brilliant minds couldn't but turn Washington into a literary center. Poetry writing had become a fad of federal employees.

This suited Sousa well. Song composing was his hobby and his weakness. To him songs stood for softness and tenderness, pent-up feelings which he never demonstrated. But he rarely succeeded in projecting his sentiments into the melodic line; his singers often complained about illogical progressions and difficult jumps. But Sousa liked to sing his songs himself. He sang with deep emotion and a hopeless crack in his voice, well realizing that it sounded awful but unable to resist the temptation. Later, when gushing fans exulted in praise of his marches, he acknowledged the compliment with formality, even indifference; but when someone remembered a Sousa song he was a friend for life.

Philip associated with literati rather than with musicians; in fact, there were few resident musicians in Washington. One of his friends was Colonel Wilson J. Vance, of the Treasury Department, with whom he had collaborated on the thanksgiving hymn for President Garfield and who now offered to write a new libretto for *The Smugglers* if Sousa would revise the music. The job was completed in practically no time.

An amateur performance in Washington, with a soldier chorus of volunteers from the National Rifles and an auditorium full of friends, was so successful that the authors decided to turn professional. Philip went to New York to hire singers, took them to Washington for rehearsals, and then on the road.

They managed to keep the operetta going for three weeks, but their funds dwindled constantly. After a performance in Philadelphia, with half of Chestnut Theater empty, Sousa went straight to his in-laws, borrowed money, and put his cast on the next train, homebound for disbandment.

It was past midnight when he returned to his hotel.

Jane was asleep. He didn't want to talk anyway. How disappointed she must be! What a flop she had married!

Yes, out of uniform he *was* a flop. He pondered unhappily. He was no good as a composer, no good as a dramatist, no good, probably, as a person. He needed the scarlet and gold, and the white stick, the paraphernalia of official functions, to cloak his incompetence. A circus fiddler, that's what he *should* have been!

Everything had been in vain. His studies, his efforts, all the trouble, all his ambitions. He remembered how a scant ten years ago Felix Benkert had helped him mark the fingering in his violin part of an Offenbach operetta, and Philip had looked up and asked, "Mr. Benkert, do you think I shall ever be able to write such an opera?" and the teacher had put his hand on Philip's head and had replied, "My boy, you'll write a much better opera than this one!" If Benkert were alive he would be ashamed of him!

He buried his head in the pillow. He was glad Jane didn't hear him sob. It didn't befit a man his age. She couldn't help him. No one could. Benkert could have told him what was wrong with his music, what was wrong with him . . .

When he awoke, a bright midday sun flooded the room. Under half-open lids he saw his wife sitting by the window sewing. He tried to crawl back under the cover of sleep, but Jane, who had seen his twinkle, dropped her work and came over to him. "Don't worry," she blew a kiss on his forehead, "it's going to be all right."

"Of course!" Philip exclaimed and realized at once that he really meant it.

He jumped out of bed. It *would* be all right. A single

66

setback didn't make disaster. Even the great had failed with their early operas. Beethoven had rewritten *Fidelio* three times. Verdi, at 27, had been heckled by an audience in Milan. Offenbach had needed his own theater because no one would produce what he wrote. So had Wagner; and he had been almost 60 when he struck it rich. Even Gilbert and Sullivan had nearly failed until *Pinafore* caught on. And Johann Strauss, idol of myriads? *Die Fledermaus* had had rough going, and without his waltz fame he'd never have made it. And most of those men depended on their music for their bread and butter; how lucky was he to wear this uniform that kept him fed and respected!

"I'll start a new opera tomorrow, and this one'll be a knockout," he said to Jane, and *The Smugglers* was already a thing of the past.

chapter ten

ÉSIRÉE wasn't precisely a knockout, but it wasn't a flop either. Edward Taber had adapted an old English comedy about an impecunious haberdasher, his pretty daughter, an old repulsive nobleman whom Father picked for her, and a nice young nobleman whom she marries. They had an excellent cast, including the famous-to-be DeWolf Hopper, for whose debut in comic opera Taber wrote a topical patter song in the Gilbertian manner, which Sousa set to music, Sullivan style. It didn't even occur to the authors that they were imitating a current fad. Native American operettas were rare; and Sousa, with some justification, fancied himself a pioneer in the field.

His first big hit was to be a march—*The Gladiators*—of which he said that it put him on the musical map. No less than 17 bands played it at a parade in Philadelphia. Published in 1886, it spread like wildfire; from coast to coast people learned to spell the name of Sousa.

President Arthur's regime had brought a new spirit into the capital. His succession to Garfield had been viewed with apprehension in various quarters and he was determined to put the gloomy prophets to shame. An ample, florid man, well groomed, courteous, and dignified, he

68

looked more like a successful businessman than the professional politician that he was. And no matter how much his opponents might resent his aristocratic demeanor, they had to admit that he was a very unusual person of high integrity and discriminating tastes.

When the President resumed official entertainment in March 1882, his first state dinner was in honor of ex-President Grant, the man to whom he owed his career. There were flowers, damask, silver, brand-new liveries, in latest New York style and quite expensive, "not a trace of the old White House taint," as one visitor wrote.

Also missing from White House routine was the Marine Band, and Sousa nearly lost his job. Arthur's private secretary had told him in passing to be ready, but failed to send the orders through the proper military channels; and while Philip sat at home, brooding why he was being by-passed, the President vainly waited for dinner music. Next morning the Navy Department and the Marine Corps office were up in arms, and the secretary refused to accept an explanation.

"The President will get a leader who will obey his orders," he thundered and pointed to the door.

In his distress Philip ran to see a senator whom he knew to be Arthur's personal friend. "Arthur's been supply chief during the Civil War and doesn't know about military etiquette," the lawmaker said. "Don't worry." The matter never came up again, but it took Philip a long time to get over his scare.

The 1883 season, too, was hectic with official and private receptions, dinners, weddings, balls, sometimes two or three a day. Early in January General and Mrs. Grant came again for a visit, and a sumptuous dinner highlighted

69

a series of entertainments in their honor. Later that month the round was repeated for Marquis de Lorne, Governor General of Canada. On Washington's Birthday, Adelina Patti, who usually never sang for less than 5000 dollars a night, performed at the Executive Mansion.

One of Arthur's sisters now lived at the White House, acting as hostess for the widowed Executive. President Arthur had a unique gift of making people feel at ease. Instead of having his guests file past a stiff receiving line, for example, he walked from group to group for informal chats. He was a gentleman in the grand manner, a "prince of hospitality," a paragon of the Elegant Eighties.

But we most resent in others those qualities which we have to suppress in ourselves. Sousa, who liked gracious living and couldn't afford it, who wanted to be boss and was responsible to a horde of petty officials, wasn't happy in this atmosphere of lustrous grandeur. Sometimes he felt as uneasy as on that long-ago afternoon at Mr. Corcoran's, and even later in life he wrote ironically that President Arthur would have done "admirably in an absolute monarchy" and that his austerity was reminiscent "of the effete aristocracy of the Old World." And he made it very plain that he much preferred Arthur's successors, even though President Cleveland hardly bothered with him and President Harrison didn't have the taste for lavish entertainment which glamorized everybody who took part in it. Strangely enough, President Arthur, who gave Sousa his first big chance, always made him feel self-conscious.

The first time he came into closer contact with the President was one evening during a state dinner, when Arthur's portly figure appeared in the doorway and beckoned him over. The band should play the *Cachuca*, the

President requested; a young lady wanted to do a Spanish dance. Sousa was sorry; he hadn't brought the music. "Oh, I thought you could do anything!" The President's voice sounded disappointed, but his powerful dark eyes were insistent. "I'm sure you can. Now, give us the *Cachuca!*" And he strode off.

Philip was getting frantic. He didn't even remember the tune. He looked at his brother. George shrugged.

"Oh, I think I remember," exclaimed a cornetist and played the melody softly. Philip blew him a kiss and bowed slightly—his favorite gesture to express approval; then he grabbed a few sheets of music paper and jotted down the parts for his first-desk men. "The rest of you, improvise!" he ordered as he gave the downbeat—and he was proud of his men and of himself at the result. He had trained them well. The group he had taken over wouldn't have gotten through the first ten bars. After the dance was over the President came out again to express his appreciation.

His term in office was almost over when it suddenly occurred to President Arthur that he didn't know the name of the tune the band always played on his arrival, and that he didn't particularly like the piece. Sousa didn't like it either. *Hail to the Chief* was a Scotch boating song, a pretentious left-over from Colonial days, selected once upon a time for its title, but lacking the martial quality which he considered imperative for a good march. It sounded odd in an arrangement for military band. No bandleader, however, had dared to break with the tradition, and no President had noticed the incongruity until Arthur called Sousa aside in the midst of a dinner party and asked him whether he considered this the most suitable air.

71

"No, sir," Philip replied, and briefly gave his reasons.

"Then change it!" Arthur walked away.

This was quite an order!

Philip stood in his study, fingers drumming on his desk, and pondered.

This was, perhaps, his opportunity.

He had felt for a long time that the Marine Corps needed a march of its own, dedicated to its motto, *Semper Fidelis*—always faithful. The corps still maintained fifers, buglers, drummers, as in George Washington's days; they weren't part of the band but Philip had written drum and bugle calls for them just the same. All he had to do was to invent a good, stirring, stimulating march, incorporate those drums and bugles, and dedicate it to the corps.

But this march had to be good. Unusually good.

What *was* a march? Or, rather, what turned a composition in march tempo into a hit?

A march corresponded to the fundamental rhythm in the human body. One-two-one-two—this was the way you breathed, you walked. A march appealed to man's primitive instincts; that's why one could be so elated by a good, stirring march.

Europeans were more complicated. They liked to escape into three-quarter time. They trimmed their rhythms and danced waltzes. They moved in circles. Americans went straight ahead.

And yet, marching was a European invention. His father had told him that it had originated 2500 years ago, in Greece. Greek tacticians had made their soldiers march in cadenced step so that their shields would move on like a solid wall. But their Persian foes believed that they were performing a war dance and looked on as interested spectators, realizing too late that it meant attack.

Sousa had often wondered why none of the great classical composers had written really successful military marches. He believed that their lives had been too far removed from the "barbaric splendor of battle." In this he was wrong. The great men of music knew war well enough; but often their countries had been at the receiving end, and defeat rarely inspires optimistic music.

A march theme had to be optimistic. It had to keep moving on. It had to be melody, not just noise. Most bandleaders were military men who only knew rhythm. But he was a musician; his musical mind worked in terms of wide, sweeping airs played on a violin. If you had a good melody, rhythm came all by itself.

The melody must appeal to everybody, even to the unmusical. It must be clean-cut, like a marble statue. No harmonic fuss. No padding. No dead weight. Or it isn't a march.

These were Sousa's fundamental theories about march-writing, which he laid down more than 40 years later in his autobiography. He also said that *Semper Fidelis* became "the official march adopted by the Marine Corps, by order of the general commanding," thus winning "official recognition by our government." This is a mild overstatement; no order to that effect can be found in the Navy Department archives. Yet the Marine Corps accepted the dedication, and by constant usage the march has become closely associated with the corps and is played at all parades and official functions. And because the trumpets and bugles made it an overly martial accompaniment for presidents placidly shaking hands in the East room, Sousa wrote the

Presidential Polonaise to replace *Hail to the Chief* at indoor affairs—a brilliant piece of salon music faintly reminiscent of Chopin.

Americans loved military pageants. Drill companies were the rage. The Corcoran Cadets, the Morton Cadets, the Washington Light Infantry, the Emmet Guards, paraded up and down Pennsylvania Avenue, and they all clamored for marches of their own.

Sousa was in his element. The National Fencibles went to Little Rock, Arkansas, for a competition and won it. Washington went wild with pride. When the victorious company returned home, Pennsylvania Station was thronged by an enthusiastic crowd. As the men reached the street, there was bandmaster Sousa raising his baton for a new march named in their honor. The band led the National Fencibles on to town. All day they paraded, and all day the band played their march, a festive piece with a beautifully melodious trio which all of Washington sang and whistled the next day.

Later in life Sousa admitted with disarming candor that, in his opinion, the main thing that made a popular hit was consistent repetition. And if the term "plugging" wasn't a household word then, he certainly mastered the technique to perfection. He got to the point where he rarely played any but his own marches on parades. No one minded, for they were good. "Even a wooden-legged man can keep step with a Sousa march," someone told him, and he saw to it that the word spread.

And, unlike many famous composers, Sousa didn't mind if his melodies were used and often misused by anyone who strummed a piano or cranked a barrel organ. He was even proud of it. "It takes a good tune to grind well," he might say. Or, "When people want to hear something again, it must be good."

In 1886, when he wrote his *Book of Instruction for Field Trumpet and Drum*, he decided to precede it with some information about music in general.

He opened with a query: "What is music?"

His answer: "Sounds pleasing to the ear."

chapter eleven

EIGHTY-NINE years after the U. S. government had moved into "the mudhole in the wilderness," Washington had become one of the most beautiful cities in America. Marshland had turned into lawns and gardens; dusty trails into wide, paved, tree-lined avenues. Public buildings majestically rose in white or green spaces. The Capitol sprawled on its hill, weighty symbol of a young nation on its flight toward world power. And the Washington Monument had risen to its imposing 555 feet, the tallest structure then in America, a landmark.

75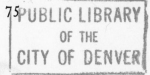

The population had tripled to 200,000 since the Civil War. The suburbs kept spreading. People of wealth and leisure built exquisite mansions amid old trees and lawns. It was a time of affluence and pomp, champagne suppers, precious furs, heavy brocades. Men of arts and letters settled in the capital which boasted the largest library and the most extensive scientific collections in the country, plus 34 newspapers and periodicals.

Competition was keen and journalism at a turning point. Until recently, newspapers had primarily been party mouthpieces, but the postwar public clamored for local news. The *Evening Star* was thriving on gossip; but the *National Republican*, desperately struggling for survival without a change of policy, was swallowed by an up-and-coming youngster, the Washington *Post*.

The *Post* had been founded in 1877 as a Democratic morning paper, but it had become politically independent when General Frank Hatton and Beriah Wilkins acquired it in 1889. Hatton was ex-Postmaster-General. Wilkins was a Congressman from Ohio. They had considerable prestige and ambitious plans: They wanted to build an entirely new audience, the audience of tomorrow.

"What do you think of our Washington Post Amateur Authors' Association?" General Hatton stopped Sousa on Pennsylvania Avenue.

Philip couldn't quite remember. The WPAAA was a new organization, he then learned, designed to stimulate the urge of self-expression among children. Its first project was an essay contest in the public schools. Twenty thousand "members" had enrolled, trying for gold medals. "We hadn't expected so many right away—but what makes you smile?"

"Thinking of three golden lyres I won as a boy . . . seems so long ago . . . I'm getting old . . ."

"Still fairly vigorous you seem to be," Hatton replied. "I hope vigorous enough to conduct the Marine Band for us, June 15, at the distribution of prizes."

The government was lending them the Smithsonian Grounds for the exercises, Hatton went on. Prominent men and women were on the committee. Mr. W. B. Powell, Superintendent of Public Schools, cooperated wholeheartedly; it was the first time that a newspaper had encouraged learning and literary expression. Yet, the celebration wouldn't be complete without the Marine Band.

Sousa said that he would be pleased to play; the General should apply to the Secretary of the Navy. As soon as he had his official order, he would come to the newspaper office to be briefed about the proceedings.

"Would it trouble you very much, Professor, if you would write a new march for us?" Beriah Wilkins ventured when Sousa called a few days later.

"None whatever. I'm used to that sort of thing."

He was looking forward to the event. Twenty thousand children—this was quite different from his usual assignments.

He knew exactly what kind of march he would write before he even got home. It didn't always happen this way. Sometimes he had to struggle for his themes; then he walked up and down in his study for hours, without writing a note, trying to put himself into a state of hypnosis, waiting for a melody to come to him. But this time it came quickly, as a happy inspiration, and, as always, melodically and harmonically at the same time. As he

77

started to write it down, everything was ready in his head but for the instrumentation.

June 15 was a glorious day. A radiant blue sky was dotted by fluffy clouds, a gentle breeze stirred the blooming acacias around the huge lawn; their sweet scent greeted Philip as he got out of his cab and crossed the gate. He headed toward the platform set up at one end of the lawn for the band, the winners, and some 160 guests of honor. His men were already seated. They looked spectacular in their bright red uniforms, white helmets, and dark whiskers, against the sun-flooded background of blue and green. He heard voices from way up, calling his name. The branches swung. The trees were loaded with boys.

At four o'clock sharp he raised his baton for the overture. People still kept coming—ladies with fashionable puff sleeves and cartwheel hats, carrying coquettish parasols; gentlemen stiff in their stand-up collars; and all around flocks of happy children. On the platform sat President Harrison's private secretary as White House representative; Colonel John M. Nelson, Superintendent of Buildings and Grounds; Justice Miller of the Supreme Court, who was to distribute the awards. In the front row were the winners, one from each grade of the District's public schools. A little girl fidgeted in her chair; she was uncomfortably dressed like an adult, all in lace and with a large hat. Next to her sat the handsome and well-mannered son of a naval officer whom Sousa knew. In the crowd around the grandstand was another of his youthful acquaintances, the Branson boy from next door; his father often came over and talked with Antonio Sousa about things musical and intellectual. Third-grader Taylor

78

Branson had competed but hadn't won; yet he enjoyed himself just the same. This was too great a moment to fret over a gold medal. He was proud to know the bandleader, and had applauded vigorously when Sousa made his bow. Little did he know that one day he would win higher honors than all the children on the grandstand and around it, that he would be in Sousa's place—Marine Band leader—and his great predecessor's intimate friend.

The overture was over. Twenty-five thousand people cheered. This was the largest gathering since the victory parade, the largest civilian gathering the capital had ever seen. Sousa wiped his eyeglasses. It was hot, conducting in the sun, when one wore full-dress uniform, gloves, and a beard. Somewhere in the crowd were Jane and their son. He looked around inconspicuously, but it seemed hopeless to spot them.

Mr. Wilkins pronounced the meeting open. The Reverend Du Corey rose and bowed his head. "Our Heavenly Father . . ." his voice carried over six acres of sudden silence.

Then Wilkins again: "The Marine Band will now play a march composed by Professor Sousa and dedicated to the Washington *Post*."

A burst of applause, cut short by an energetic chromatic progression.

A new era of popular music had begun.

A light, tripping theme, in 6/8 time . . .

The 6/8 tempo was unusual for a march. Sousa had already used it in *Semper Fidelis*, however. It sounded pleasant and festive. There was something of a dance step in it, something that gave a lilting touch to the forward motion; it brought a dash of humor into the march, and

79

elasticity which, for him, was the life of a composition. It had something an ordinary march was bound to lack: charm.

Small feet began to tap the lawn.

The lively theme was followed by a sweeping broad melody—loud, as a march should be, slightly trivial, and extremely effective. Then came an abrupt drop into gentleness—a new theme, a lyrical monologue first in piano and repeated full blast so it could be heard all over the field—woodwinds shrieking in highest pitch over choirs of cornets, saxophones, horns. A last massive chord in C Major folded into cries of enthusiasm—children's voices rising like piccolos over a roar of applause.

The piece followed the standard pattern of the military march: introduction, first strain, second strain, trio, "break," and coda; yet nobody in the audience felt that they had heard such a thing before.

Sousa played the march again on the dress parade that afternoon, and at the Arlington Hotel in the evening. He played it over and over again, as he did his other marches, until people whistled it in the streets.

Yet this was nothing unusual with a Sousa march. The most extraordinary thing about *The Washington Post* seemed to be that it was dedicated to a newspaper. Whenever a band marched past the *Post* building, it played the tune. But they played other new Sousa marches as well: *The Thunderer, The Loyal Legion, The Piccadore, Ben Bolt;* and, above all, *The High School Cadets,* which he wrote after reading that public schools in Philadelphia encouraged the use of music, but that pupils were assembling and dispersing to an imported tune, *Old Heidelberg.*

And Philip went about his routine, playing at concerts or on parade, for important guests and less important fans, outdoors, indoors, sometimes slightly frustrated by the sameness of his service, then again stimulated by public acclaim. On July 3, he wrote down the definite score and sent it to his publisher. One more march, like all the rest.

And then it happened. Somewhere in the U. S., a dance band struck up *The Washington Post*. Slightly bewildered couples started dancing to a Sousa march.

Three gliding steps to two counts of music, blended as if they were one—this was the two-step. It had be danced as smoothly as a waltz, but quieter. The ladies, with torturing stays in their collars, tight corsets, heavy draped skirts, sighed relief; so did the gentlemen in burning patent-leather shoes and starched shirts. Until now they had scorned the two-step; compared with the waltz it had seemed dry and boring, until *The Washington Post* pepped it up. The accent on the second part of the measure actually suggested syncopation, the intriguing, strange new rhythms to which Negroes now danced on the stage. *The Washington Post* was the answer to the dancing masters' prayers.

The dancing masters of America had formed an association several years before to purge dances of postwar vulgarity. But when they had completed the process, they discovered that all color and life had gone too. Listless couples stalked across dance floors in a systematic succession of prim and complicated steps; or rather, they sat around dance floors, discouraged and bored. Sousa's march worked like a magic potion.

Some people objected that a march was a march and not a dance. The dancing masters convened and pronounced *The Washington Post* a two-step. And they agreed that the two-step could be danced to *Semper Fidelis* and *The High School Cadets* too.

Sousa's marches made the two-step fashionable. And as the Elegant Eighties slid into the Gay Nineties, they revolutionized social dancing, sounded the death knell to the waltz. When Eduard Strauss, the Waltz King's youngest brother, toured the United States with his band, he noted irritably that Americans had forgotten three-quarter time. Thanks to Sousa, they danced the two-step to the lilting tunes of Johann Strauss. Regardless of what the orchestra played, boys and girls shoved across dance floors in the rhythm of *The Washington Post*.

The Washington Post carried Philip's name and fame across the oceans. In Borneo an U. S. Army officer heard a small native boy play it on the violin, with the sheet of music pinned to a tree in the jungle. In Germany an orchestra played it during the dedication of a Wagner monument. In France an American heard a little peasant girl play it on the piano. When Philip and Jane were in Venice, a music-store clerk told them that Giovanni Filipo Sousa, whose *Washington Post* had just been played on the Piazza di San Marco, was one of the most famous Italian composers—though not as famous as Maestro Verdi yet, for he was still quite young.

All over Europe the march blared in dance halls and on ice rinks, the first piece of American music that swept the old continent long before the invasion by jazz. People actually had forgotten that it was a march, and hardly anyone knew that it carried the name of a newspaper. They called the two-step *The Washington Post*, and thought that it had something to do with the post office.

82

The march sold 1,200,000 copies in the first five years. The man who grew rich was not Sousa, however, but Harry Coleman, the publisher, who eventually bought two factories on the proceeds from Sousa marches. In 1886, after an unsuccessful attempt to get as much as 50 dollars for *The Gladiators,* Sousa had signed a contract with Coleman, under the terms of which he would sell him his marches, in three arrangements, for a straight fee of 35 dollars apiece!

chapter twelve

M Y OBJECT in those days was not to make money but to build an enduring name," Sousa dismissed the matter years later. And he implied that, having always lived in modest circumstances, he wasn't aware of the absurdity of the arrangement until much later, when he was too rich to care.

Something else bothered him far more: hard as he tried, he couldn't get raises for his men or a commission for himself. He was also refused permission to take the band on tour. Colonel McCawley obviously felt that public funds shouldn't be used for such ventures, and every time Philip broached the subject he got a flat no.

The band wasn't even permitted to substitute for Gilmore's at a coveted commercial engagement, at fashionable Manhattan Beach. At best McCawley would allow one-day furloughs to play in Richmond, Baltimore, Philadelphia; and official out-of-town assignments were few and far between. Yet Sousa wanted to travel. He *had* to travel in order to build his name. He wanted to play his music across the country. He wanted to show what he had accomplished with a band of enlisted Marines. He grew increasingly bitter, for he felt he was being let down, morally and financially.

In 1888 he had bought a house, at 318 B Street, a two-story structure, with four rooms to each floor. The living room was in the front; to the rear was his study. It was a rather small room with one large window overlooking an alley green with trees and shrubbery. His desk stood beside the window; it was a good place to work.

Elizabeth Sousa and Philip's oldest sister, Tinnie, came over to get Jane started in the household. They hired a maid, who assumed full control. Jane never learned how to run a house and she never bothered with such masculine concerns as bookkeeping and cash. She was strictly Victorian in her interpretation of a woman's job, and having married so young she never had a chance to shed the chrysalis of her Philadelphia education. She was always a little helpless and never on time; "the late Mrs. Sousa," friends started calling her when she was in her mid-twenties.

The stocky, swarthy Philip and the white-haired Jane

84

with her fair skin, coal-black eyelashes and her dresses in pastel colors, set heads turning wherever they went. Their personalities, too, were attractive contrasts that blended and never clashed. Sousa's closest friends claimed that no one ever saw him laugh. He mostly was serious and poker-faced; but people who knew him well said that he laughed with his eyes, which narrowed to a slit when he enjoyed himself. He spoke little, in brief, measured sentences and with a slight croak in his voice. But Jane kept chattering away. She had a lighthearted, sunny temperament. Whatever Philip said was all right with her and she hardly ever made a suggestion except in pettish matters in which she could be quite insistent. "Mother has the temperament, father has the talent," the children would chant in unison.

Her absolute, unquestioning faith in him amused Philip sometimes. He didn't always believe that he was so matchless a musician, so faultless a person, so great an intellect, as he seemed pictured in his wife's mind. Yet it supported him a great deal, strengthened him in critical moments, helped to develop his staidness, judgment, and initiative, which made him far more than a bandmaster and march composer, but one of the greatest musical figures of his time. When their tenth wedding anniversary approached, Philip asked his old collaborator Edward Taber to write him a suitable lyric for the occasion. *You'll miss a lot of fun when you're married,* Taber produced. Philip's eyes narrowed to a slit as he presented the song to Jane, and she laughed heartily and said she hadn't missed any.

Philip was always able to snatch a bit of leisure. His hours were irregular, but the band didn't work too hard. Unless he played for an official engagement, he came home

85

for lunch. Whenever he had business in town, he stopped at Billy Wagner's store on Pennsylvania Avenue, main gathering point of the Washington male. Billy Wagner sold sporting goods, and his customers met in front of his store, as they might assemble at the post office in a small village and talked guns, quail, flies, and baseball. Billy himself was one of the best shots in the country, the idol of shotgun and rifle amateurs.

Often leisure meant more music. In Philip's living room stood an old and inexpensive "tin panny" square piano; here on free evenings he rehearsed with Washington's musical youth whom he had organized into an amateur chorus for Sunday night performances. On hot days the Negro children listened outside the open front door.

He also liked to read. He had inherited from his father both his curiosity and his quick perception. Rows of books lined the walls of his study. He would check the source of any unfamiliar word and unknown fact. Even a casual family conversation might wind up around a pile of dictionaries. He was constantly filling the gaps in his knowledge and in Jane's, and he trained the minds of his children as soon as they knew how to spell. "My fondest memories are of our family dinner table, where our conversation roamed over every possible subject, and where the solid brilliance of Father's mind would strike sparks from our own," his daughter Helen reminisced more than 20 years after his death.

When Philip first realized that the position of Marine Band leader had no real standing, he was deeply shocked. He saw that he had made a mistake in assuming that it carried prestige. The leader had seemed omnipotent while Sousa was an apprentice. He also might have obtained the wrong impression from his father, who, often absent because of his asthma, had to be very humble to court good will. But once Philip was on the leader's stand, it dawned on him that he was but a glorified noncom. It was Sousa who gave the band its later status by virtue of his professional excellence, his personality, and the slightly pompous bearing he acquired to compensate for his youthful age.

From his second White House concert on, the band was served regular meals in the State Dining Room. Before, they had been deprived of their refreshments by disdainful waiters, maids, and guards; a test of strength with a haughty footman, and a subsequent interview with Mrs. Hayes, had done the trick.

It had been an uphill fight all the way, yet his personal success was impressive. In 1885, when a group of journalists founded the Gridiron Club, they voted Sousa a life member and musical director, a distinction which the Marine Band leader holds to the present day. Band members might rebel against his perfectionism and his aloofness, but he was on the best of terms with persons of consequence. Major George Porter Houston, the commanding officer of the base, insisted that no program of American music could be any good without a Sousa march. Colonel Dan Lamont, President Cleveland's private secretary, was a personal friend. The British Embassy had made a habit of borrowing the band on Queen Victoria's birthday; and whenever foreigners were entertained aboard the presidential yacht, Sousa was requested to play.

On one of such occasions, in 1889, when 17 foreign countries were represented, Philip obliged by playing the national anthem of every single one of them. He had spent hundreds of hours of his own time collecting and arranging foreign anthems, and always kept them on hand. Pleased and surprised, Secretary of the Navy B. F. Tracy suggested that this collection be completed for publication, which Sousa promised to do if he could get government backing. Published in 1890, this official volume, a standard reference work for many governments, was another feather in his cap.

This assignment gave Sousa a great deal of trouble. It had been one thing to get the anthems of countries like Denmark, Russia, Germany, Sweden; it was another to dig out Indian songs, typical melodies of, say, the Cherokee and Dakota, the Eskimo and Apache. Sousa found ethnologists and travelers who sang the tunes for him, then he gave them proper harmonic treatment without changing one note of the melody. Airs from distant places, Abyssinia, Lapland, and Samoa, the East Indian and Fiji islands, found their way into the volume which grew into a folksong anthology far beyond its original goal. He wondered why the largest countries had the shortest anthems, and why anthems grew in length the smaller the countries were. He counted 14 measures for the British, and 16 for the Austrian, but 70 for Uruguay, and a full 144 for the republic of San Marino, a 38-square-mile dot on an Italian mountain slope.

Working on those songs, imagining landscapes and the strange peoples whose fates and peculiarities were captured in them, increased his urge to travel. Before his inner eye rose wide plains and forbidding mountain ranges, rivers, lakes, and canyons, odd colorings and shapes—and he didn't even know his own country, had never been west of Chicago and St. Louis, was held in fetters by red tape and a red uniform. At such moments he loathed his job.

Sometimes he stayed away for days in a row, leaving rehearsals and concerts to the assistant leader.

Then, late in 1890, Colonel McCawley fell ill. Now Sousa, who had hesitated to by-pass the man to whom he owed his job, felt free to suggest a Marine Band tour directly to the Navy Department. Secretary Tracy was sympathetic and sent him to see the President. And Sousa, whom the Washington mills had ground into a first-class diplomat, went to see not Mr. Harrison, but the First Lady.

Harrison had been considering a personal good will trip, it turned out, but when his wife spoke to him about Sousa's idea he decided that flamboyant uniforms and rousing marches would be more effective than a lone man in mufti riding by in a cab. That much he told Sousa as they were standing at a huge window in the White House parlor, overlooking the Potomac valley.

It was decided that a professional manager should handle the tour. David Blakely of Chicago was the logical choice. Then Sousa engaged a lady soloist, Marie Decca. It seemed odd to have a soprano sing with 50 military bandsmen, but Gilmore was doing it with much success; for his European tour in 1878 he had taken on an unknown young girl from Maine, one Lillian Norton, who soon made her debut at La Scala, as Lillian Nordica . . .

Blakely had handled Thomas and Gilmore for a number of years, and the previous summer he had imported the Eduard Strauss orchestra from Vienna. He was no ordinary impresario, however. He was a rich man with a hobby— onetime secretary of state of Minnesota and president of the Minneapolis Philharmonic, who had turned printer and publisher in the 1880's, and possessed King Midas'

89

gift of turning into gold whatever he touched. Within a few years the Blakely Printing Company of Chicago had grown into one of the most prosperous concerns of its kind in the country. Investing part of his growing fortune into orchestras and road shows, he considered the Marine Band one of his lesser clients and had the bookings made by a man from his New York office, Howard Pew.

Sousa got almost dizzy when he saw his schedule. The tour was to last five weeks. It would start on Wednesday, April 1, 1891, with a matinée in Bridgeport, Connecticut, and an evening performance in New Haven. On the second day they would play Worcester, on the third Boston, on the fourth Providence. Then they would cover upstate New York, proceed to Akron, Cleveland, Detroit; spend their third week in Michigan, and a week end in Chicago. Then Iowa, Nebraska, Illinois again, one week in Indiana and Kentucky, back to Ohio, returning via Pittsburgh, and winding up in Washington, on Monday, May 4.

There were no concerts on Sundays, but even so, it was an eight-to-nine-concerts-a-week proposition. Sometimes they were booked in four different towns within two days, which meant traveling between matinées and evening performances, and again in the morning. Invitations for luncheons, dinners, banquets, receptions, poured in even before they left. This would be the most strenuous affair he had ever gone through, far more than his road tours when he had been, alas, 15 years younger. Yet the President's bandmaster couldn't snub the civic groups determined to honor him.

Sousa, in turn, was determined to startle his audiences. He hitched a large saber to his belt to emphasize the military element, and played concert classics. The marches on the program were from operas like *The Prophet* or *Aïda*, or even the "Procession of the Grail," from *Parsifal*. When people clamored for his own marches they got them as encores; but first he made them sit through Wagner, Bizet, Liszt, Berlioz, through Grieg's *Peer Gynt* or Schubert's *Unfinished Symphony*. Sousa indulged in music no band except Gilmore's and his own could play well. He reveled in the sounds of his symphonic poem, based on the Chariot Race from the novel *Ben Hur*, in which he imitated hoofs, wheels, and scythes. Toward the end of the program he might turn humorous; one of his hits was a Humoresque called *Good-by*, patterned after Haydn's *Farewell Symphony* and making fun of the state of affairs in the band: tired of the leader's nagging, the oboe leads the exodus of rebellious bandsmen, playing *I'm Going Back to Dixie*, and similar farewell songs; but irked by the conductor's indifference and realizing that payday approaches, they precipitately march back to duty, repenting with *Annie Laurie's* dulcet air.

They had packed houses and rave reviews all the way. Yet travel was still extremely uncomfortable. Trains might be hours late. Food was poor; some sections of the country through which they passed weren't equipped to serve balanced meals to transients. And he had never enough sleep. Shortly after he reported back to home duty he broke down, exhausted from overexertion. The navy doctor insisted that he take a long vacation, involving a change of environment. He suggested Europe. Jane relished the idea.

And so one month later they were on the high seas. It was Philip's first acquaintance with the ocean; the man who had spent most of his life as a marine knew it only from boardwalk promenades.

The elements were not kind to the Sousas. On their third day a cotton cargo caught fire during a storm so severe that the passengers were alerted to abandon ship. Their cabin was burned out completely, and flames kept eating away at the vessel for the remainder of the trip. When they finally saw another steamer and signaled for help, its captain dropped dead from shock.

A few days after arriving in London, Sousa forgot the address of their boardinghouse and nearly got lost.

Later, in Bayreuth, he stood at Wagner's grave, and in Paris, he saw a Bastille Day parade. And yet, his own account of his first trip abroad doesn't give the impression that he was affected by what he saw. He doesn't mention the brand-new Eiffel Tower, then the tallest building in the world, standing 985 feet high; or Buckingham Palace, Westminster Abbey, or the Thames Embankment—not even the performance of *Tannhäuser* part of which he heard in Wagner's theater. His story revolves around people and how they received him: the French Minister of the Fine Arts who had praised his song collection, an American consul who had been impolite, the difficulty of getting tickets for Bayreuth. He made an ironic remark about the pompous cavalry escorting the carriage of President Sadi Carnot of France, and thought it wonderful that President Harrison preferred to walk alone, even in bad weather. It almost seems as if he had built up a shell of resistance to keep from being overly impressed.

Fundamentally, however, Sousa was not narrow-minded, nor did his patriotism turn him hostile toward foreign things. He merely refused to be impressed by strangeness for strangeness' sake, and he bided his time to understand the Old World which he knew so well through its music.

Had he made the trip when Mr. Corcoran offered to send him, he might have returned an epigone of musical neo-Romanticism, a pilgrim who had lost his creative roots. Coming when it did, his first trip abroad made him conscious of the fact that he was a representative of musical Americanism, and that his best talents were home-grown.

"One never feels as patriotic as when under a foreign flag," he often said.

chapter thirteen

HERE we've got something that should be worth a million to you," Coleman said and handed Sousa a magazine.

It was a brass-band journal published in England. The best military bands now came from America, it said; and "Sousa, conductor of the government band in Washington, is entitled to the name of March King quite as much as Strauss is to that of Waltz King."

March King . . . Waltz King. . . . Sousa . . . Strauss . . . not bad!

"Look what we're doing," Coleman showed him the draft of an ad: "You can hear his music from the Atlantic to the Pacific, from the St. Lawrence to the Gulf Stream. The March King reigns supreme."

Philip suppressed a sarcastic remark. Yes, March King was worth a million—to Coleman!

He pocketed the magazine and took it home to show it to his father. Antonio read the article, then slowly, circumstantially, read it to his wife. "Why *shouldn't* they call him March King?" he commented. "He's a prince in his own right."

Philip thought of it as he bid his father farewell in March, 1892, to take the band on its second tour of seven weeks from coast to coast. He thought of it again as he mounted the podium in Chicago and made his slight, jerky bow to the audience. In the auditorium he saw the prominent features and funny, overlong goatee of David Blakely. This was the first time after he had taken over that Blakely heard a concert by the band.

At this time Blakely was an angry man. Even more: he was disgusted.

The International League of Musicians was pressing for a bill to prevent foreign bands from coming over and competing with home organizations, and they pointed at Eduard Strauss as their prime target.

Blakely didn't want Congress to tie his hands, even though managing Strauss hadn't been strictly pleasant. First he had had to prove that Strauss' men were "artists" —not mere "musicians" whom the Union might not have permitted to land. Then Strauss' boat had almost been put in quarantine because a Polish baby had died of measles; as long as he lived Blakely wouldn't forget that afternoon

94

in Hoboken, when he had watched the proceedings with a telescope, realizing that thousands of dollars were at stake. Strauss himself had been a problem. He had kept fretting about travel conditions and restaurants, and in New York he had collapsed from heat prostration.

Blakely finally decided that he needed a hardy military man, and had spent a summer in Europe, trying to sign up a famous bandleader like Wettge, the Frenchman; or Komzak, the Austrian; but neither could get leave of absence. On his return he had booked Sousa's trip; but two days before the Marine Band was scheduled to leave Washington, the St. Louis Musicians Union had stirred up protests against the official band competing with "local talent." They hadn't been able to prevent the trip—but Blakely had had enough.

He scrutinized Sousa carefully. Here was a very unusual conductor. He stood nearly motionless, like a sentinel; only the slight quivering of his saber showed that his leg muscles moved to the music, that his whole body was alive with rhythm. His arms didn't make one unnecessary movement. His conducting was clean and sharp; it almost seemed to leave a trace in the air. His eyes were strong; when he looked at a player, the man couldn't possibly miss the cue. He did a lot of conducting with his eyes, unnoticeable to the audience; and the lively, brilliant music evoked by the quiet figure was extremely effective. But when the coda came, when the woodwinds shrieked in the highest registers, the brass blared, and the percussions thundered, his arms swung up and down, like Indian clubs, and the audience was thrown into hysterics. This effect, however, the "Sousa swing," was reserved for his own marches which he played as encores. Very clever not to put them on the

95

program, Blakely thought; let the audience ask for them.

As Blakely sat listening, his quick mind was thinking. This man combined Wettge's genius for drill with Komzak's elegance, and he was second only to Gilmore in personal magnetism. He was better than Gilmore, as a composer. He had authority, he was young, healthy, good-looking . . .

". . . If you can create such a success for the Marine Band, why, then, couldn't you do it for Sousa's Band? Have you ever thought of having a band of your own?" he asked next day at Philip's hotel.

"No," Sousa said curtly and unconvincingly. He had often dreamed of a band of his own, of hiring whom he pleased, doing as he pleased; but he had never permitted himself to dream for more than five minutes.

"No," he repeated after a pause, watching Blakely carefully. He hardly knew the man.

He couldn't think of leaving Washington, he explained. He had just settled down in his house. His father was ailing. And he had a family to support. He couldn't afford to give up a lifetime position, retirement pay, and all . . .

"Would you do it if I could get it financed?"

"I might think it over," Philip said evasively.

Whereupon Blakely released a statement to the Associated Press that the President's bandmaster was considering an offer to form a concert band in Chicago, modeled after the organization which he had led for the past 12 years.

Philip read it en route and was annoyed. This premature, wholly unfounded announcement might get him into trouble. Unfounded? He realized, almost with a shock, that he was pleased. Blakely really had done him a favor.

He *did* consider leaving Washington; he *had* had enough; and they might just as well know it.

There was no use beating about the bush: his job had come to a standstill. It was gratifying to perform at the White House, to watch history in the making—even if one were sort of tucked away in a corner. He had experienced great moments, General Grant's funeral, for example, the most solemn thing in which he had ever participated; and the dedication of Washington Monument. There had been speeches and a brilliant parade. The Marine Band had been "in attendance." Mr. Corcoran, his voice slightly pitched by 87 years of wear, had delivered the key address. Mr. Corcoran was a self-made man who had started very humbly and worked himself up by sheer courage and energy.

But the March King was still making 1500 dollars a year—less than a White House clerk!—and hesitated to give it up. Blakely would probably offer more. It might mean a career. But where was security?

He was tired of having to leave Jane behind when he traveled. It irked him that she could never hear him perform unless she rubbed shoulders with the crowd. She was never invited to official functions. But Mrs. Swallow *was* invited; he had seen her palish face at a White House reception. The Swallows—Corcoran—here was a social gap he should be able to bridge at long last!

Security was well and good; but where was his career?

All over the country young people were on the move, trying to make good. Washington was expanding; but weren't there natural limits to the capital as an artistic center?

He pondered as the tour went on. He pondered past

97

cornfields, and canyons, and glaciers, through deserts and blooming meadows, and lush dark woods. At every stopover he collected fan mail telling him about the storm which had been unleashed in Washington by the mere insinuation that he might leave. So much the better, Philip thought; if they gave him a commission, he would stay.

It almost seemed as if Washington were split into two camps fighting over Sousa—the ones who called Chicago presumptuous and snapped that it would want the White House next; the others who called the government stingy and wanted Congress to vote Philip an increase. The Washington *Post* thundered that Sousa's departure would spell the end of the band. The real issue, however, went far deeper than the departure of a popular citizen or the loss of an able public servant. The issue was Chicago.

The big Eastern cities were proudly watching westward expansion, yet they didn't want their cultural assets to migrate. And they were getting jealous of Chicago, the bustling new metropolis that had risen from the ashes of the big fire. Within 20 years Chicago had become the second-largest town in the country, with mushrooming industries, 35 railway lines, 24 theaters, and no less than 531 publications for its 1,208,669 inhabitants. The Eastern cities watched the upstart as a flock of swans might watch a duckling transforming into an eagle. Now Congress had chosen Chicago as the site of the mammoth Columbian Exposition and World Congress, even though Washington, New York, and Brooklyn had vied for the distinction to commemorate the fourth centennial of the discovery of America. Already workmen had converted 666 acres of marshy lake shore into a "White City"—150 exposition buildings made of a new material that looked like marble.

There would be a solemn dedication around Columbus Day, 1892. Theodore Thomas, as musical director, would conduct. A music committee negotiated with Antonin Dvořák and Ignace Paderewski. A chorus of 1500 was being assembled. Gilmore would be there. Blakely, so far, had nothing; he needed a new attraction, a sensational attraction—and time was running short.

All this, however, Sousa didn't know. To him, it all boiled down to a very personal problem which, for the time being, he dismissed from his mind. On April 6 they arrived in San Francisco for a four-day engagement at the Opera House. San Francisco was an acid test; he anticipated rough going. People were grumbling about Blakely's high prices, and they were very partial to their local Park Band, which played triweekly, gratis. "We are so accustomed to good military band music, that [the Marine Band] will have to play mighty well to be an attractive novelty," Sousa read in the *Musical Courier*. This didn't sound encouraging.

They did play mighty well, however. A long review in the San Francisco *Argonaut* compared Sousa with his most famous colleagues and rivals and came to the conclusion that none of them, quick or dead, foreign or domestic, had done better than Sousa and his Marines. "Mr. Sousa's troupe is one of which any conductor might be proud," it said.

He *was* proud of his men as he read this. They were indeed as this writer said, "a band of soloists," and yet "parts of one great machine." Their precision work, the way every one of them responded to every nuance in his conducting—it was going to be hard to train a new band; he would have to start from scratch. And the result? From

99

a glorified noncom he might turn into a glorified tramp. He fingered the badge on his cap—brass eagle perched on an anchor, clutching the hemisphere. If only he could get a commission! He'd much rather stay!

He wished he could talk it over with his father. Father always knew best. He hadn't been much of a moneymaker in his day, but he had done well by his sons. As their route switched back toward Chicago, he decided to find out exactly what Blakely had to offer and not to commit himself until after his return.

On April 27 they played in Duluth. Sousa was bowing to a cheering crowd when he saw the local manager wave a bit of paper. He waited until the curtain fell. The paper was a telegram. Father was dead.

Mother requested him to continue the tour and not to disappoint the public.

How could he conduct cheerful concert music in this frame of mind?

He pulled himself together. A disciplined trouper and public servant had to go on with the tour. Never must he disappoint the public. Father would have wanted it so.

A matinée in Oshkosh, Wisconsin; an evening performance at Fond Du Lac. The following day back in Chicago. And now he had to make his decision all by himself.

"How much does the government pay you?" Blakely asked.

He certainly knows it, it flashed through Philip's mind. He could have spared me the embarrassment. "Fifteen hundred," he grumbled.

"How would six thousand, plus twenty per cent of the profits, suit you? A few businessmen and I might form a syndicate and hire you on these terms."

Six thousand—this sounded too good to be true—he wished he knew more about business . . . where was security . . . ?

". . . under a five-year contract . . ." It was as if Blakely read his mind.

Thirty thousand dollars minimum in five years—more than the government would pay him until retirement.

And Blakely also hinted that he might publish Sousa's compositions, with excellent terms.

Blakely continued talking. He was suave and persuasive. He painted rosy pictures of a bright future. And he was extremely flattering.

With Gilmore about to retire, Sousa had no competitor, he claimed. There were still Cappa, Brooks, Dan Reeves of Providence, Rhode Island—old gentlemen of the old school, time-beaters without imagination. Blakely would promote him with a bang, at the dedication of the Exposition buildings; and throughout the summer Sousa's Band would be the major attraction at the Fair. And Chicago was only his springboard; he would become the most popular conductor in the world, on a par with the very great in music. . . .

"You have the talent," Blakely urged. "Ambitious young men don't stay home; staying means stagnating. . . . But you can't wait much longer . . . the time is now . . . don't get buried alive in your pretty home town. . . . The world must know you, and you must know the world . . ."

". . . I hope you have confidence in the success of our Blakely Amusement Company," he interrupted his own harangue abruptly.

"Why . . . yes . . ."

"Good! For we expect you to buy some stock; a thousand dollars would be adequate."

Sousa hadn't intended to invest hard cash in himself, but Blakely's drive was irresistible. Before he had even seen his own contract, he held 1000 dollars' worth of stock in a syndicate which could operate only if he obtained his release from the government!

He applied immediately on his return but had to wait until the end of July. By then he was so anxious to leave that he hardly read the final draft of his contract and didn't even notice that he signed away his library and half of his royalties from compositions written during the period of the partnership!

A citizens' committee headed by the Secretary of the Treasury and notables from both Houses of Congress arranged a formal testimonial for him at the National Theater, July 29. Next day Sousa led the Marine Band on parade on the White House lot for the last time. A quick-step march—*The Washington Post*—and then farewell. Farewell to the uniform, farewell to the bugle calls on the tiny parade ground to which he had been accustomed since childhood, farewell to the barracks with the old arcades through which, once upon a time, Father had led him toward his vocation. He was getting sentimental. Father! What would he have said to the great change?

"Yes, Philip ought to have his own band, it's time for him to go," Antonio Sousa had said; but the family hadn't told Philip; they wanted him to make up his own mind.

A great change it would be—a life of hotels, furnished apartments, restaurants, trains; separation from the children as they grew old enough for boarding school; separation from his widowed mother.

The house was closed down and much of the furniture given away. Sousa's eyes clouded slightly as the movers shoved his desk into a van—the desk at which he had written the marches that had crowned him king.

chapter fourteen

L ADIES AND GENTLEMEN, your attention, please." The manager's gravity raised apprehension. "I have a solemn duty to perform. Patrick Sarsfield Gilmore is no more . . . He died at six forty-five this evening. I am sure that you all share in the deep sorrow . . ."

A confused murmur filled the spacious auditorium of the St. Louis Exposition building where Gilmore's Band, that night under assistant leader Charles W. Freudenvoll, was playing for the eighth consecutive season. Only the night before, September 23, 1892, the "Prince of Bandmasters" had scored another triumph.

A banquet had been held in his honor after the concert; there were formal addresses and informal compliments; a ladies' committee had given him a globe of hothouse flowers three feet in diameter, and it had caused a good deal of hilarity when the cabbie refused to put it on top of the coupé lest it strike electric wires, and wrestled for half an hour to get it inside. Animated and cheerful, Gilmore had returned to Lindell's Hotel and talked with his wife and daughter until long after midnight, chuckling in retrospect about his awkward little speech of thanks. At two-thirty in the morning, he had felt stomach pains; by five, the doctor came, and insisted on calling in two specialists, but later in the day Gilmore became delirious and all efforts to save him were in vain.

A few minutes after the manager had spoken, the auditorium was deserted. "Gilmore dead!" a newsboy yelled from the steps of the Exposition building, while dazed concertgoers stood in the corridors, and the band made its exit as if under a spell. Outside, in the dressing rooms, some of the older men broke down and wept like children.

Gilmore had been in poor health intermittently, but during the last year he had seemed well. He had settled down somewhat after his mammoth festival spree; his home on 164 West 86 Street was among the most luxurious on New York's fashionable West Side, with a valuable library and a roomful of trophies and souvenirs.

Occasionally his old adventurous spirit had stirred him into trying just one more sparkling spectacle; only last New Year's Eve, at midnight sharp, he had struck up his band at City Hall to welcome America's quadro-centennial year with a serenade of sacred and patriotic music and 30,000 New Yorkers had gathered to listen on the cold, wind-swept square.

In the spring he had met a former schoolmate and was

visibly irritated at finding him looking old. "How come you keep so young and sprightly?" the man had asked him as if he had guessed his thoughts, and Gilmore, strangely relieved, had retorted, "Time beats us all, my dear friend, but I beat time!"

And now time had caught up with him forever, and he lay dead in a hotel room, the globe of faded flowers a ghastly symbol of the fallacy of earthly things.

Two days later, in Plainfield, New Jersey, a stocky, bearded bandmaster raised both hands to stop applause, then opened the first concert of his new band with the mournful strains of Gilmore's *Voice of a Departed Soul.* This was more than symbolic; it had a touch of the theatrical which no one would have relished better than Gilmore himself. At their dress rehearsal that morning "Sousa's New Marine Band" had adopted formal "resolutions of sorrow and respect," one of them stipulating that this piece would open every concert on their maiden tour. A gesture to the memory of the deceased—one era of band music fading into the next. "The Prince of Bandmasters" was dead; long live the March King!

Sousa's New Marine Band, as Blakely had blithely called the new outfit, wore semimilitary uniforms, navy blue and braided in black, with velvet collars, somber and high; only Sousa's own dress tunic had a little gold. Twice during the program, the cluster of dark-clad men was lit up by two bright spots: the lady soloists who appeared in pastel shades, as Jane liked to wear them. The formal black dress which they at first inevitably brought along disappeared at the bottom of the trunk after the first concert; Sousa hesitated to interfere officially in such private matters as a young lady's podium gown, but ladies in black could not help but notice his long, cool, silent, slightly disgusted stare.

The size of the band was to vary through the years, adapted to the nature of each tour. When traveling a great deal, through many small towns, he would naturally hire fewer men than for a protracted stay in New York. In the beginning the band numbered 49—a hand-picked cosmopolitan lot: a British cornetist snatched from the Coldstream Guards; a bass drummer from the Guarde du Corps in Berlin; the clarinetist was Italian, the flutist Scotch, the bassoonist a temperamental Frenchman called Jambon, which means "ham." There was an array of Germans, and there were even some Americans like Arthur Pryor, the superb trombonist.

Salaries started at 35 dollars a week. Contracts provided that musicians had to rehearse two weeks without pay before the tour, that they could be dismissed for incompetence on a two weeks' notice, and fined or fired for absenteeism or "ungentlemanly conduct" even off duty. Sousa would not allow substitutes and he would not grant collective requests, but he promised to investigate grievances, presented in writing, within a week.

No longer hamstrung by red tape and official regulations, he indulged in the pleasure of rehearsing as he saw fit. He was more of a military man than he realized, and more of a perfectionist than ever. It was a problem, of course, to forge into one concise, sonorous body musicians who were strangers to each other, playing arrangements which were new to most of them. To obtain a full round tone, Sousa wanted musicians of each section to play exactly alike. He started the first rehearsal by making the clarinet

106

soloist play the opening bars, first merely the notes, then the same passage with proper modulation and wind control, over and over again, until it sounded perfect. Next, he requested the assistant clarinet soloist to play it exactly like his partner.

"That's impossible, sir," the man objected. "No two players play alike."

"Try it!"

The first demonstrated, the second imitated. Gradually the tone qualities of the two clarinets became indistinguishable. This procedure continued through the entire section, then switched to others. By luncheon recess Sousa's Band had mastered 16 bars of some light overture.

The men's first contracts ran for a nine-week tour, interrupted by a fortnight's rest. The first leg of the trip would take them to the Middle West, highlighted by two weeks in Chicago—the two crucial weeks which should establish Sousa as the country's leading bandmaster. A "Grand Formal Opening" at the auditorium was to last six days, to be followed by concerts at the dedication of the Exposition buildings. Then, after their vacation, they would play New England.

The band arrived in Chicago on Monday, October 10, and Sousa immediately started rehearsing the big *Columbian March* by Harvard's John Knowles Paine. After a while the hunchy figure of Theodore Thomas appeared in the auditorium, and Sousa yielded him his place on the conductor's stand. Thomas would lead, in a monster performance, the joint forces of his own orchestra, Sousa's Band, and a chorus of 5000.

Sousa's thoughts drifted as he sat with Blakely in the front row, listening at the same time with intense concentration. Only a few short months before, Blakely had promised to put him on a par with the greatest in music, and already he was collaborating with Thomas, remote idol of his boyhood. Would Chicago really launch his new career? Was this a good omen, or merely beginner's luck?

Strange how similar his early experience was to Thomas', it occurred to him that night, after a luncheon to which the conductor had invited him and which had lasted until dinner. Thomas too had joined a band as a mere child, when he had been second horn player in the Navy Band. He too had fiddled in dance halls and orchestras, substituted for an opera conductor at a moment's notice, and eventually exchanged the violin for the baton. They were both promoting great music of their own time: Thomas via the symphony orchestra, Sousa with attractive arrangements for a more popular medium. But while Thomas was opinionated and uncompromising in his efforts to build an educated audience, Sousa considered himself the public's servant whose duty it was to please, to entertain.

The dedication ceremonies were set for October 21, a big international affair. The day before, Chicago's Civic Parade took place; Sousa led the huge column of 75,000, marching 20 abreast, past a reviewing stand on which sat a brilliant gathering of notables from Washington and Springfield, and from abroad. And because "Sousa's New Marine Band" was a concert organization, "definitely" and "positively" not available for parades, its name was "Sousa's Chicago Band" for the day. Sousa marveled at Blakely's cunning and watched him with the sober interest of a mature learner.

Had he still doubted that his new enterprise constituted a promotion, he would have been reassured on the following morning, when his old Marine Band, 50 men strong, led by his successor Petrola, paraded on official duty. They marched unspectacularly near the tail end of a long array of soldiers, passing in review before the guests of honor, and then vanished from the scene. But he, Sousa, would open the ceremonies as soon as those same guests would have gathered in the Administration Building, the largest structure ever erected under roof, covering nearly 30,000 acres, seating half a million. The notables sat on a huge raised platform, with flags cascading around them and a gigantic stone eagle spreading its wings overhead. The 100,000 invited guests looked quite forlorn in the immensity of the hall.

"Rising like a flood of melody to drown the senses," an eyewitness recorded, Sousa's New Marine Band played the prelude to the greatest international affair the country had ever seen.

But the six months' period between the prelude and the actual show of the great Fair, was punctuated by trouble. The government, as could have been foreseen, objected to the name of "New Marine Band" and, detached from its old affiliation, Sousa's name alone wasn't the drawing card it had been expected to be. The New England tour started ominously. Business was reasonably good in places Sousa had played with the Marines, but poor where he was unknown.

Sometimes, when he took his bow, he was appalled at the long stretches of empty seats. He was getting ever more restive as they moved on. A conductor could only give concerts as well as he knew how; the rest was up to the impresario. And Blakely had booked him in the wrong territory, that much he knew.

The impresario joined the band in Boston late in November. But before Sousa could give him a bit of his mind, as he had intended, a poker-faced Blakely asked him to his room. "We're losing money," he said curtly. "I'm closing down that tour as of tonight."

"You won't!" Sousa shouted. It was one of the few times in his life that he lost his temper. He suddenly remembered what Theodore Thomas had said to him at that luncheon in Chicago: "Managers will stick close when you are making money, but they'll desert you without a qualm when the first squall blows up." He wanted none of the experience of the always-struggling, always-losing, celebrated Thomas.

His face was a bluish red as he accused Blakely of blundering and mismanagement, of wanting to ruin his career, of making a laughing stock of him in Washington, and all over the country. But he wasn't the person to be closed out, not he! he roared. The band had two more weeks to go, and two more weeks they would be playing.

The torrent came to a sudden stop. Blakely shrugged well-tailored shoulders. "Well, if you insist, Bonnie Boy . . ." The nickname Blakely had given him sounded outright offensive in this atmosphere. Their leave-taking was cool, but the band moved on.

Business picked up during Thanksgiving week. Yet a scar remained. Sousa could never forget that Blakely had been ready to scrap him, without batting an eye, at the first disappointment. He had no patience with poor losers. But soon he had to admit to himself that he couldn't have found a better impresario.

One by one, the late Gilmore's engagements went to Sousa. As the members of Gilmore's Band bickered amongst themselves over future leadership, Blakely had quickly snatched from them their most important regular engagements—the exclusive resort of Manhattan Beach for the summer, the St. Louis Fair for early fall. This would not make friends for Sousa among bandleaders, but if one wanted to get on in the world, strong enemies were as important as good friends.

Actually, pandemonium had broken out in Gilmore's Band almost immediately after the leader's death. It had caused Mr. Corbin, owner of Pennsylvania Railroad and the Manhattan Beach theater, to bow out of Mrs. Gilmore's parlor after a visit of condolence without mentioning further business, and to give the 18,000-dollar contract to the up-and-coming man.

In Gilmore's Band four vociferous German players clamored for the conductor's job, and the Board feared that if one of them were chosen, major trouble with the others would result. So the Board and a players' committee decided to approach a complete outsider, and their choice fell on veteran bandleader Dan Reeves.

"Knowing you to be the only man in America worthy of keeping the band up to its high standard and following in the footsteps of the lamented Gilmore, we extend to you, Sir, a hearty welcome and support," Reeves read with astonishment, in Portland, Oregon, where he was conducting his own band at the Industrial Exposition. He had never fancied himself Gilmore's peer. Sousa, too, was surprised at the turn of events when he read a reprint of the telegram in Chicago. He hadn't given much thought to Gilmore's successorship, but it made odd reading that the elderly gentleman should be called the *only* bandleader in America worthy of the honor. Sousa didn't like it at all.

Immediately after finishing in Portland, on October 23, Dan Reeves hurried to St. Louis to meet the band. But precisely what the Board had wanted to prevent, happened. The infuriated Germans banded together and started large-scale sabotage. Americans could not beat time, they claimed, and dramatized this statement by playing out of rhythm until chaos ruled.

Reeves, a heavy-set, gray-mustached, dignified gentleman, had never faced such a situation before and vainly tried to cope with rising disorder and spreading resistance. And as the months went by, and Gilmore's Band deteriorated from concert to concert, its best players resigned their jobs. Next thing Reeves heard was that the deserters, including two men who had been on the committee which appointed him, had climbed on the bandwagon of John Philip Sousa. Only a few months after Sousa had started his band, all of his first desk men were highly experienced, Gilmore-trained veterans.

Early in 1893 an open letter reached the offices of the *Musical Courier*, which the editors reprinted in the issue of March 15. Gilmore's Band had opened attack.

"A persistent effort is being made," the opus charged, "by interested and unscrupulous parties . . . to silence [Gilmore's] great name, to create the impression that Gilmore's Band is no more. . . .

"A syndicate was formed, headed by a man whom Mr. Gilmore repudiated for reason. A gentleman and a musician was induced to leave a prominent position under the government and a band selected haphazard from various parts of America was hastily formed, purporting to hail from Chicago, for the avowed purpose of running Mr. Gilmore from the field."

The letter graciously "acquitted" Sousa of "any intent except to make as good a band as possible"; but it elaborated on Blakely's alleged misdeeds, claiming that, having had to drop the name of "New Marine Band," he was trying to hang on to Gilmore's coattails by hiring some of the 2000-odd musicians who had played under the lamented master at one time or another, and was now relying on the reputation of "a few fossiled and worn-out members of Gilmore's Band."

The lengthy document bristled with insinuations and half-truths, exaggerations, inaccuracies; it was quite unworthy of Reeves who undoubtedly had drafted it, and it turned into a boomerang. An editorial called the letter "of equally bad taste and business tact," "a wrathful plaint over the loss of Gilmore's engagements and Gilmore's best men"; it actually questioned the band's title to continue calling itself Gilmore's.

The "fossiled and worn-out members of Gilmore's Band" also spoke up. They circulated printed cards stating that they had been Gilmore's well-advertised favorites who had joined Sousa because they considered him an accomplished and exceptionally successful leader whose long engagements promised continuous work.

A pathetically short note by Reeves in the next issue of the magazine—a few angry remarks about deserters breaking their pledges for "better jobs"—seemed to have ended the matter.

Except for some caustic remarks Sousa kept aloof from it all. He felt sorry for Reeves, a musician of 30 years' standing, suddenly faced with the impossible task of acting as Gilmore's successor without Gilmore's engagements and Gilmore's best players, and without the good will on the part of the remaining ones. Had there been any truth to the accusation that Sousa's infant band was out to undermine its famed rival organization, public and professional opinion might have swung against him with fatal results. By then, however, most people knew of the internecine struggle in Gilmore's Band which had started the chaos, and the drastic manner in which Reeves tried to save face created considerable resentment. Blakely experienced with glee that nothing can be more helpful to a publicity-conscious person than being subject to denunciation. While he blithely ignored their false accusations, his enemies gave Sousa's band the best promotion it could have had.

On April 16 the band shared Carnegie Hall with Walter Damrosch's Symphony Orchestra—another first, another triumph. The New York *Press* called it one of the chief musical organizations in the country. On May 5 Sousa conducted a Columbian Festival in Boston, his men being reinforced by a ladies' symphony, a large chorus, and Metropolitan Opera soloists. Then Buffalo, Detroit, St. Louis, Omaha, Minneapolis—and finally back to Chicago, to the Exposition on which Blakely had pinned such high hopes.

Six American bandmasters and four from Europe gave 14 concerts daily, on stands and in pavilions located at strategic hubs within the intricate network of roads and paths that crisscrossed the grounds. There were other musical attractions—Welsh, Mormon, Polish, German, Russian, Swedish choirs; ensembles from Java, China, Samoa, Korea; oratorio festivals, organ and children's concerts. Walter Damrosch brought the New York Symphony, Franz Kneisel the Bostonians. Yet the big crowds went where Sousa was. The papers wrote that the other bands combined drew about as many people in a week as he played to every afternoon, and the space around his pavilion was always like a big island in a stream of milling humanity. One day, when the choral director of the Exposition ventured that Sousa's public would like to sing with him, Sousa swung into *Swanee River* and the grounds reverberated with an impromptu chorus of many thousands. Sousa repeated the experiment whenever he felt that his public was in the mood, and the prospect of audience participation yet increased the attraction.

"The one musical success of the World's Fair was made by Sousa's Band," the Chicago *Herald* stated, and later, summing up: "One blast from Sousa's Band was worth more to the Exposition than all the bands the management could furnish in a year."

Basking in glory, Sousa went on to Manhattan Beach, to St. Louis, then on a nation-wide tour; this was to become routine for a number of years. At Manhattan Beach, a resort of two hotels, an amphitheater, and a concert pavilion, he found some leisure for family life and composition. He was careful to live up to his growing reputation of being more of an artist than Gilmore, but did not want to disappoint old-timers accustomed to Gilmore's stunts. So, while he rationed the use of artillery that Gilmore had lavished on popular favorites, cannon still thundered the rhythm when Sousa closed his concerts with the National Anthem.

The 1893-94 season was a succession of new high points in his career: Ziegfeld's Trocadero in Chicago, the San Francisco Midwinter Fair, New York's Madison Square

Garden. Here, by popular demand, he topped his engagement with an all-Sousa program, playing some of his early waltzes and overtures; old march hits and the newest ones, *Liberty Bell* and *Manhattan Beach*, the latter a revision of an old exit march written for Nobles; also no less than three orchestral suites: *Sheridan's Ride*, *The Chariot Race*, and *The Last Days of Pompeii*, all in one concert. He was particularly proud of the latter; five years later, when asked which he considered his best work, he answered without hesitation, "The Pompeii Suite, which I never published. It is a descriptive composition and I prefer it to everything else I have done. Some of the orchestral effects had never been invented before I hit on them— particularly the suggestion of terror that I get by means of the trombones."

In 1895 he marched into Atlanta, Georgia, where the Cotton State Exposition adopted his *King Cotton* as the official march. The fair was in sore straits when the band arrived but Sousa's public appeal saved the day.

In between were stopovers in little towns and concerts in the vicinity of wherever he happened to be staying. They played under tents or under wooden structures or under the open sky; in opera houses, concert pavilions, and amphitheaters; on grandstands and platforms, on lawns and boardwalks, and between gravel paths. There were always color and movement around Sousa, flags, lampions, torches, milling crowds, and novel effects brought forth by that young marvel, electric light. Sousa developed an obsession of moving on. A few days of rest and he longed for the road, keeping as best he could his family life from disintegration. The older children were in boarding school, but Jane and little Helen would occasionally come along or meet him somewhere for a lap of his trip. Travel was strenuous. Trains were slow and untidy. Helen might fidget during long stops in the middle of nowhere, and boss the bandsmen into getting out of the train and picking flowers for her to trim her hat.

In wintertime, of course, it was much worse. Trains were unpredictable; and sometimes, despite advance arrangements, no transportation to the concert hall was available. Thirty or 40 trunks containing the heavy instruments might be piled up on the snow-covered platform, with 30 or 40 apathetic musicians standing around, trying to protect their fingers and lips from the cold. The men playing the smaller portable instruments hurried on to the auditorium. To their ever-renewed amazement, Sousa was there ahead of them. His presence of mind and practical approach to unexpected problems kept him from becoming alarmed over situations beyond his control. In such emergencies he might start a concert with a dozen men, relying on their ability to improvise, and the band kept swelling in size and sound, as horns, basses, trombones, drums, and their shivering players straggled in.

The public hardly ever lost patience. When once, on their way to Butte, Montana, melting snow and broken bridges stalled their train, a packed audience waited for three hours to hear them, and they started the concert, numb with fatigue and hunger, at 11 o'clock at night.

Yet Sousa was happier than he had ever been before. He was pleased with his music, pleased with his audiences, pleased with himself. And pleased with Blakely.

Blakely drove him hard. Spectacular ads as might have plugged a Barnum attraction advertised "Sousa's Peerless Band." Its leader's fame was plastered all over the country and his face became more familiar to the people than almost any other American. And as his compositions swept households and dancing schools, orchestras, bands, pianos, barrel organs, and even the infant phonograph, he was quickly getting rich. Already he was making more money than any government official except the President of the United States.

In 1895 he heard from DeWolf Hopper again, who remembered with fond nostalgia his and Sousa's earliest trials and errors in *Désirée*. Meantime Hopper had founded his own company and sent his manager, B. D. Stevens, to his old friend Philip, with a libretto by Charles Klein; if Sousa would consent to write the music, he, Hopper, would produce the work.

Sousa liked the story of *El Capitan* well enough to not only write the music but also help put some prose into verse. The plot dealt with a Peruvian uprising against the Spanish conquerors, interwoven with romantic intrigue. One of Sousa's earliest attempts at poetry, *The Typical Tune of Zanzibar*, rescued from oblivion and set to music on the train from Omaha to Chicago, became one of Hopper's hit songs.

With Hopper playing a hero compelled to lead the forces of the enemy against his own, and his wife Edna Wallace Hopper in the female lead, *El Capitan* opened on April 13, 1896, in Boston. Some critics were lukewarm, but for the public an operetta by Sousa was a natural attraction and everybody raved about the march, a centerpiece of particular brilliance and luster.

For many years, Sousa would claim later, *El Capitan* vied in popularity with the Gilbert and Sullivan operas, among theatergoers on this side of the ocean.

chapter fifteen

OUSA was alone on the windswept deck as the SS *Teutonic* steamed into open sea, homebound from Liverpool. It was a blowing, nasty November day in 1896. Everything was gray and desolate. Even the fog horn sounded as if muted by a wet muffler. The sea was choppy and quivered with impatience.

Sousa paced the dripping deck, his cap pulled deep over his eyes, the collar of his heavy coat turned up. He walked steadily, his gait briskly cadenced despite the roughness of the weather. He was thinking.

It was good, he thought, not to be disturbed by a staring crowd who expected one to do something spectacular. They did not understand that it wasn't easy being a composer and bandleader, that even a March King had worries. He faced them now, in an appropriate frame of glumness.

He and Jane had been on a long vacation, traveling incognito. But the sovereign in the realm of marches could not always go unnoticed, and he and Mrs. Sousa were occasionally recognized. London, Paris, Vienna, Italy, Switzerland. He had seen people who could not always understand his language but danced and marched to his melodies, and hummed them as the most familiar of sounds. The trip had been pleasant while it lasted—until this abrupt, bitter end.

On the last Sunday of the Berlin Industrial Exposition he conducted the Philharmonic Band. It had been a chilly, overcast day, and during the concert the heavens spilled rain on the audience. Yet the soaked listeners held out on soaked grounds, huddling under whatever umbrellas they had, fumbling with wet programs, shouting and applauding Sousa with a display of temperament quite uncommon in Prussia. The Berlin press, hard to please and proud of its sophistication, had called the Sousa numbers "poems in march rhythm." The popularity of America rose to new heights. The American Embassy wined and dined him, even though he was no longer in government service and had plainly registered as "bandmaster from New York." He had done well by his country.

Sousa stopped at the afterdeck. The Stars and Stripes stood stiff in the breeze, as if cast in colored metal. Yes, he thought, I have done well by the flag.

He resumed his walk. Blakely had written that the Berlin concert had created a sensation at home. Fan mail, newspaper clippings piling up. David Blakely! You might disagree with him, argue with him, but when it came to business he was all right. He had been right about Sousa from the start. He had made him the most popular bandmaster in America, and his band the best, his audiences the biggest—in a mere four years.

And now Blakely was dead, and Sousa's Band had no manager.

This was the source and object of Sousa's troubles, and the cause of his precipitated return.

As long as he lived, he would never forget the past few days: the piercing shock when, lazily at breakfast in Naples he saw an item in a four-day-old newspaper from Paris that the well-known New York impresario David Blakely had been found dead in his Carnegie Hall office, felled by a stroke; his frantic telegram to Blakely's assistant Frank Christianer, and Christianer's laconic confirmation of the news; the cancellation of his plans to visit Sicily; the hectic journey to Liverpool to catch the next boat. Jane never mentioned her disappointment. She was a good companion, a good wife.

He too would have wanted to stay. He would have liked to hear more music in Europe. He merely had a smattering of it—an overwhelming concert under Hans Richter in London; a disappointing performance of Suppé's *Boccaccio* in Florence; an unforgettable rehearsal of the famed, venerable choir of the Vatican in Rome. But now he had to concentrate on business. His band was waiting. He would have to make the most important decisions all by himself. He was responsible for some 60 men and their families, in addition to his own.

Still the flag stood stiff. But a melody came up from the waters beyond. It rose, and floated around the Stars and Stripes, and forced him into step with its rhythm. It was a good, an inspiring, melody . . . but how would he make out without Blakely, as a guide and troubleshooter?

There was a good deal of trouble ahead, he knew. Pat Gilmore's Band, salvaged by the up-and-coming Victor Herbert, triumphed again. They had snatched back from Sousa the coveted engagement in St. Louis and were now stumping the continent as in the days of yore. Herbert did have a manager, who worked from Steinway Hall, just across the street from the Blakely office, like a mole in the dark. Then there was Innes' Band, advancing by leaps and bounds; Blakely's own unfaithful Howard Pew promoted this upstart outfit from Chicago, brazenly calling it the "greatest popular music band in the world"; they were even talking about a European tour, which would precede a similar undertaking by Sousa by at least one year.

Europe. . . . The flag seemed to point back to it, but the dim outline of the coast had long dissolved in grayish haze. "No," Sousa said to the flag. "Forward! Not back!"

There was another continent ahead of him—America, home, the country of the flag, the good land in which he, and Gilmore before him, had planted the seeds for good band music. He would not concede. He would hold his ground in the land of the flag. Forward the ship went. Onward he would go.

But, having nowhere else to go at the moment, he toured the promenade deck with quickening step. He was all alone in a world of water and clouds—gray, grim, cruel, a world without color and form.

Out of nowhere the melody re-emerged, soothing, cheerful, strong. The ocean sang it to him, in its steady, eternal beat. He stopped and looked up. In the world of water and clouds there was the flag towering above, streaming against the tumultuous sky, the steady pole in a drifting universe, a guidepost.

The Stars and Stripes . . .

     . . . the gem of the land and the sea . . . waving forever . . .

Eternal was that flag, like the motion of the sea, the drift of the clouds. In his ears droned a band, playing that same melody, on and on . . . it soared high, enveloped the flag, and the Stars and Stripes fluttered slightly, as if in response.

The melody remained with Sousa, disturbed and worried as he was throughout the trip. It was with him as the *Teutonic* docked in her home berth. It stayed with him during hectic conferences which determined the future of the band. It was a faithful companion that never distracted him, but waited patiently until he paused, and then it would surge forth, a stream of comfort and confidence, a source of power and trust.

Christmas crowds that year saw huge posters announcing that Sousa's Grand Concert Band would start the season in Carnegie Hall, on December 27, and from there go on a nation-wide tour, covering 21,000 miles, "from ocean to ocean, from gulf to gulf"—the most ambitious trip ever undertaken by an artistic organization.

This was the astonishing results of Sousa's endeavors, the fruit of his sweeping optimistic energy. There was little time left between preparations and rehearsals; but on Christmas Day he stole away from the family gathering and wrote down the melody: he needed a new march for the tour. And as it stood there, in the rigid musical symbols, he couldn't help but wonder whether people would realize that this was far more than another Sousa march—something very special and personal—his hymn of confidence. 1896

He called it *The Stars and Stripes Forever.*

Americans hailed it at once as an inspiring, most extraordinary melody; and its magic effect was not limited to the citizens of the country whose flag it glorified. A Frenchwoman once said that it created in her a vision of "the American eagle shooting arrows at the *aurora borealis.*"

Experts claim that *The Stars and Stripes Forever*, with its sweeping and iron optimism, represents the most stirring musical expression of patriotism, and they rate it among the best military and patriotic marches ever composed. They also discovered that this was the first piece in which certain bandsmen rose and moved to the front of the stage to play certain passages—a Sousa invention later widely applied in jazz.

The effect was overwhelming. Sousa the showman fully exploited the dramatic potentialities furnished by Sousa the composer. In Philadelphia's Willow Grove Park, for example, where the band would play later for many millions of people through many summers, six trombonists lined up in front of the audience when the trio came up, and as it surged forth, in a mighty crescendo, a huge American flag was unfurled in the background, to a crescendo of glaring reflector light. People raved, carried away by patriotic enthusiasm. They almost choked with excitement as the theme roared along in the horns and trombones, with piccolos and clarinets adding flourish and brilliance. Their emotions were stirred to a pitch by the bright blaze of sound and color. The love of their flag had found a new expression.

The creator of *The Stars and Stripes* was not only rewarded by acclaim. The march, equalled in popularity the world over only by Johann Strauss' *Blue Danube* waltz, netted him an unprecedented 300,000 dollars in royalties.

Foreign visitors often would rise when it was played, believing that it was the National Anthem.

Actually, in 1914, San Francisco schoolteachers adopted a resolution asking that *The Star-Spangled Banner* be replaced by *The Stars and Stripes*. And even though no such revolutionary change was even considered, schoolchildren have come to associate with Sousa's piece Fourth of July and other patriotic celebrations. On March 10, 1932, a few days after Sousa's death, Representative Lichtwanger introduced a bill in Congress (HR 10369) "designating the musical composition 'The Stars and Stripes Forever' by John Philip Sousa, the national march of the U.S.A." The bill was referred to the Committee of the Judiciary, and ordered to be printed.

The Stars and Stripes remained Sousa's own favorite, the most vivid expression of his noblest feelings, his mark of identification.

Once in Buffalo, when he wanted to cash a substantial check but carried no piece of identification, he turned his back to the window, raised his arms, and began to conduct in his own peculiar manner, whistling *The Stars and Stripes*. The hilarious acclamation by everybody present convinced the cautious teller that the serious, bearded gentleman was no impostor.

On another occasion, in South Africa, he stopped at a roadhouse restaurant near Kruegersdorp. The innkeeper carried a victrola out to the front porch and played Sousa marches, as crowds of natives assembled. Then he asked Sousa to join him outside, told the gathering who the foreigner was, and played a record of *The Stars and Stripes*. The crowd salaamed, pressed forward to touch his coat and hand; and so insistent was their appreciation that the innkeeper had a hard time extricating the celebrated guest from his admirers.

In 1912, the band gave a good-will performance in the Atlanta penitentiary. The warden drew Sousa's attention to a somber, mean-looking individual who, he explained, had been sentenced to death for several murders; the sentence had been commuted, however. The murderer remained impassive throughout the program; but as the first bars of *The Stars and Stripes* were played, his expression changed, his rigid figure relaxed, and afterward he applauded vigorously.

The Stars and Stripes Forever has gloriously outlasted Sousa's worldly life. It still stands a symbol of two of the finest American traditions—energy and optimism in an emergency—which have inspired its composition.

chapter sixteen

THE era of Sousa!" a musical journal raved in 1896. This sounds strange in retrospect, what with Brahms, Bruckner, Verdi, still alive, young Richard Strauss already shocking our elders, Mac-Dowell holding the fort in America, Debussy, Mahler, Delius, Dvořák, in their heydays. And yet, for the American public at large—the unsophisticated, melody-loving, rhythm-happy crowd—the era was Sousa's.

When he returned from Europe, he found *El Capitan* going strong and everybody clamoring for more of the kind. *The Bride Elect, The Charlatan, Chris and the Won-*

derful Lamp, followed within three fertile years, and, after a lengthy interval, *The Free Lancer* (1906)—the best stage work he ever wrote, according to contemporaries.

The Charlatan was another operetta commissioned by Hopper who eventually introduced it and *El Capitan*, also in England. The other three were staged by Klaw and Erlanger, the fabulous producers of the Gay Nineties, who lavished upon *The Bride Elect* all their luxurious and expensive imagination. The try-out took place in New Haven during Christmas week. Three months later *The Bride Elect* was the most profitable operetta production in the United States.

This gave Sousa particular satisfaction for *The Bride Elect* (originally called *The Wolf*) had been his problem child *par excellence*, with a record of a solid dozen turn-downs. Sousa had kept working on it on and off during his Marine Band days, writing his own lyrics for the first time, and then sent it out to practically every star and producer he knew. Some had kept it for months, but ultimately the bulky package had returned to its hearth like a faithful kitten. "Unsuitable for production by anyone but a speculator," was the consensus of polite rejection. The eminent Andrew McCormick added angry comment: "You have violated every known principle of comic opera production!" Later Sousa felt inclined to view this as a compliment.

But when after the success of *El Capitan*, Klaw and Erlanger contracted for a new Sousa operetta with most favorable terms and for the earliest possible production, the composer, who did not like any of his efforts to go to waste, took the dormant *Bride Elect* off the shelf. He was counting on Charles Klein to fix up the text; but when even Klein shied away from the hopeless opus, Sousa took it along to Manhattan Beach to give his old characters a new plot and some new music. He worked on it all summer, between rehearsals and bicycle rides, forsaking social engagements, spending his spare time in his suite in the west wing of the vast hotel, into which no sound penetrated but the whistle of the local train and the eternal song of the sea. The producers received the finished product in the fall, as Sousa had promised.

The reception of the work was mixed, however. Some reviewers found Sousa jokes silly and wondered why on earth he had turned playwright. They didn't quite know what to think of pearls like:

> "To marry or not to marry
> That is the interrogation,
> Whether a husband will be to me
> A joy or a complication."

"It is so easy *not* to write lyrics!" one critic remarked. Another thought he recognized familiar shadows in the music—Meyerbeer in an *a cappella* Invocation, and Berlioz in a sprightly tarantella; but he hastened to add that he did by no means insinuate plagiarism. A third arrived at a more respectful conclusion: the March King had probably aimed at a travesty of grand opera.

Actually, the plot, about an imaginary Italian monarch who wages war over the slaying of a favorite goat, might have turned into a fine vehicle for topical satire in the hands of a Gilbert or Offenbach. Sousa had taken his text very seriously, however, and he resented those who did not appreciate his sense of humor. "My jokes are aimed at the average audience," he retorted. "I don't propose to publish diagrams to make people understand them!" But hadn't he avoided knockabout horseplay? Hadn't he blazed new trails in comic opera? For example, he had tried to suggest an Italian atmosphere by writing a recitative 15 minutes long; and in the first finale he had the curtain fall on a moonlit empty stage, after the night watch with lanterns had solemnly walked across. That much he said in an interview, and it is not quite clear whether he had never seen *Meistersinger*, or was poking fun at the reporter, or really thought that he could get away with such a fantastic statement 30 years after Wagner had established the precedent.

However this may be, whether Sousa wanted to imitate or to ridicule, and however hard he tried to make the most of his lesser talents, the transcending feature of this new operetta was and remains a march, placed at a strategic spot, the second finale. The melody had occurred to him on the evening of July 4, after an exhausting, sweltering holiday's work. He had completed it that night, and the one number written in a few hours' time stole the show. When a soldiers chorus in flashy uniforms paraded onstage in six-eight time, even those who disliked Sousa's stiff efforts to be funny, cheered the creator of their favorite rhythms and inspiring melodies.

The spell of Sousa's name, the march, and the spectacular production counterbalanced whatever damage reviewers might have done; and since Sousa collected for both music and libretto, "his royalties were largely in excess of any ever paid to an American composer," according to *Metropolitan* magazine.

To many people Sousa was the symbol of the American patrician. Latin grandezza, American largesse, Victorian deportment, and an innate flair for a good effect had blended into an exceptional personality. A picture from these days shows him at his desk, wearing the velvet jacket of the 19th-century father, starched shirt, and boots with unusually high heels to make him appear taller than he was. His luxuriant beard had been trimmed to moderate size, his mustache was longer than before and drooping, his hairline showed an inclination to recede. He looked older and more sedate than a gentleman in his mid-forties, and the solemn seriousness of his expression hardly seems to belong to a person whose purpose in life it was to spread enjoyment, to stimulate, to entertain.

Eighteen thousand bands now played his music. Sousa marches seemed part and parcel of national celebrations here and abroad. In 1897, when troops paraded before Queen Victoria on the occasion of her 60-year Jubilee, the united bands of Her Majesty's household brigade struck up *The Washington Post*. The British had great marches of their own, but evidently none that matched Sousa's swing and dash.

Sousa had often thought of taking his band to England, and in 1897 when Colonel Mapleson, the British impresario, brought his opera ensemble to New York's Academy of Music, Sousa invited him to a concert. The rest was simple. An elaborate tour was quickly arranged and announced. Colonel F. W. Hinton was hired as a publicity manager and advance agent. They expected to create a sensation, even considered performing opera—*El Capitan* —with a British cast supported by Sousa's Band!

But then Spanish-American relations reached the breaking point and anti-American feeling abroad caused Mapleson to suggest postponement. Meantime the Gilmore forces had recaptured Manhattan Beach and Sousa had no commitment for either spring or summer. He remained unperturbed, however. While his manager made tour arrangements, he quickly put a showpiece together, *Trooping the Colors*, a dramatization of patriotic songs of the United States and friendly nations.

In Scottish garb and playing bagpipes, his choristers pranced through the aisles; they played *Yankee Doodle*, clad as Continentals; donned British uniforms for *God Save the Queen*; they shouted the *Marseillaise* in accented French, and danced in Cuban costumes. Throughout the show 200 hand-picked girls and young men grouped and regrouped themselves in spectacular tableaux. And when the men, in Marine blue, finally lined up to salute the Stars and Stripes, and a radiant beauty clad as Columbia led the singing of *The Star-Spangled Banner*, audience enthusiasm reached fever pitch.

Patriotic demonstrations were frequent and ardent in those days, but, according to an eyewitness, none matched the one at Sousa's concert at the Metropolitan Opera House, on April 10, two weeks before the declaration of war.

A new generation had come of age since the Civil War. The wounds had healed, but the scars had not completely vanished; and in sensitive times the theme of unity was struck up fortissimo to stir the reluctant. When Sousa's Band swung into *Dixie* right after the National Anthem, rebel yells and Union cheers filled the house; a man leaped from the Diamond Horseshoe into the aisle, shouting that everybody was ready for war, and another roared that the North and South stood united for flag and country.

Sousa too wanted to serve flag and country. Immediately

131

after war broke out, he volunteered to join the Sixth Army Corps and organize regimental bands. But virtually on his way to Camp Chickamagua he was struck by typhoid fever that outlasted the war. He received the Headquarters Badge just the same, as a full-fledged member of the armed forces, acknowledging the fact that his absence had been considered sick leave and not failure to report. A captain's commission, however, for which he had been hoping, did not materialize. Evidently President McKinley and the War Department did not see why a man who had been in service with the explicit understanding that his assignment did not warrant promotion should be commissioned just because he had *left* the service and was doing well by himself. Bandleaders never rated all too high with the brass.

But while illness kept Sousa out of active duty, his marches led men into action. When Dewey's squadron sailed up the bay to attack Manila, the band of the flagship SS *Olympia* struck up *El Capitan*. It was *El Capitan* again that saluted the hero of the Philippines on September 30, 1898, in New York, when he reviewed the now-historic great parade from a grandstand in front of Washington Arch. Sousa himself led the Olympia's band, augmented by his own, down Riverside Drive and Fifth Avenue; he had insisted on making an exception in order to honor the admiral, his friend of long standing.

Sousa had become the most sought-after entertainer in the country. Every march he wrote turned into a dance hit. Every statement he made was quoted, interpreted, paraphrased. Ladies gushed, ex-soldiers shouted moist-eyed hurrahs, cigar wrappings bore his likeness, cartoonists and comedians thrived on his foibles. Sometimes he received letters addressed to "The March King, U.S.A.," or even with nothing but his silhouette as identification.

Sousa anecdotes circulated in tearooms, drawing rooms, taverns. He now indulged in the luxuries he had coveted as a young man. Fans who crowded his greenroom during intermission found a superbly trained valet in attendance. When the Sousas took a summer house, they were served by their old Washington maid and her entire family. For a number of years he took a boxing coach along on tour; he was seen in the company of both Bob Fitzsimmons and John L. Sullivan, whom he had met at the gymnasium of ex-champion Jackie Cooper, where he practiced.

In New York he also became a familiar figure on the bridle paths of Central Park, having taken up horseback riding after his illness, on doctor's orders and with characteristic ambition. After only one year of horsemanship he rented a mount in Los Angeles to visit friends in Pasadena, and was almost thrown in front of a streetcar when the animal shied away from a brass band. Later, however, he would often take long horseback journeys without incident, mostly in the fall when he went hunting, or when he was in Virginia or Philadelphia, and wanted to visit his mother in Washington. His companion usually was ex-cavalryman Ed Shannon, whom Sousa left in charge of his horses and dogs when he was away. For a number of years he maintained a kennel in Henderson, North Carolina, where his hunting headquarters had been established on the farm of ex-Mayor Dick Sutherland. But while his passion for hunting was gradually superseded by that for trap-shooting which did not involve the killing of living creatures, his fondness of horseback riding continued to his ripe old age, even after his horseman's career had been climaxed by a 1000-mile horseback journey undertaken at the age of 62. Trotting along fields and hillsides, taking short cuts over meadows, picking his way through underbrush, ears and eyes impassive and relaxed, he rediscovered nature's rhythm, detected hidden music in the singsong of wheat, in the murmur of a breeze. Many a good strong melody was born on those long, silent rides.

His concert repertory was unusually large, yet he kept hunting for new or unfamiliar gems in private and public libraries. He could score a popular tune more quickly than five copyists could write out the parts. For his programs he usually listed nine selections but was prepared to play 36. The nine were arrangements of other composers' music, the remaining 27, Sousa originals. Only when he had a new hit or symphonic poem did it figure on the bill. Encores came after every number; a jerky bow after Wagner, Schubert, Puccini, Berlioz—applause cut short by a vigorous downbeat, and the band would plunge headlong into a Sousa march. Rival musicians hollered "bad taste." Here and there an earnest reviewer opined that Sousa was striving for cheap effects, debasing art. But the fact remained that people came to hear the music that was not listed.

First Sousa's march tempi followed army regulations of 120 beats a minute, but gradually increased to 136. He never yielded to the temptation of speeding up in off passages, slowing down in soft ones; crescendos must not be agitated, trumpet figures never slur. Monotony could not be avoided by irregular rhythms, but only by proper accents within the strict time and by variety of instrumentation; players must not waste their breath on unaccented notes, and not even a short strain must be played the same way twice.

Sousa got the most unusual effects merely by muting brasses or cutting out certain instruments. For the accompaniment of soloists he toned the band down to woodwinds, harp, and the lightest brass. In the singable trio the clarinet usually carried the melody, very occasionally yielding its dominant place to the baritone horn (*El Capitan*), but often with fanfares added for extra brilliancy. He boldly used the saxophone, previously barred from symphony orchestras and concert bands because its sound was considered too sad. Sousa made a clear distinction between scoring for concerts and for parade; if he published the concert version, he usually added cues for brasses to replace the woodwinds when marching.

To improve the sound of his band he even turned inventor. He found that the Helicon Tuba (that brass giant curling around the marcher's body, with the weight resting on his shoulders and a large bell blaring the music far ahead) was not well suited for the indoors; its frontal attack was too powerful. So Sousa suggested a new type whose bell could be turned up, so that, as he said, "the sound would diffuse over the entire band like the frosting on a cake." The firm of Wurlitzer & Company made the instrument to his specifications and called it the Sousaphone.

Sousa hardly ever played his marches exactly as they were printed. Explaining that any good parade march had to be "dressed up" for concert performance, he achieved the widest possible circulation with a simpler official version, while reserving his best effects for himself. Usually, episode and coda were played "as written," but he silenced piccolo, oboes, cornets, and trombones in the first playing of the second strain and the beginning and end of the trio.

This pattern became known as the "Sousa style," but it was only a basic pattern to which he did not religiously adhere. Variation, improvisation, and unpredictability were basic elements of the Sousa thrill.

Not even veteran players like Herbert Clarke, Arthur Pryor, and others who eventually left him to found their own bands were able to conduct a Sousa march in proper Sousa time, and with the swing and the dash that rang in their ears. Bandleaders the world over wondered about the "Sousa secret."

There was one man who believed he had found the key to the riddle—tuba player Emil Mix, Sousa's occasional sparring partner. Facing him in the ring, Mix noticed that Sousa's arms were unusually short. These short arms made him conduct a trifle faster and enabled him to keep the tempo to the end, while others would have tired or fumbled. A slightly accelerated rhythm became his second nature, gave his performance its unparalleled vitality and verve. But Mix did not brag about his discovery, and if Sousa was at all conscious of this factor in his conductorial uniqueness, he kept the knowledge to himself.

chapter seventeen

THE problem of management kept bothering Sousa for a long time after Blakely's death. Even though determined to seize the reins of his business, he still had to rely on the people who handled it. But his depressing experience with Blakely's heirs made him wary of partnerships.

Right after his return from Europe, bursting with sympathy and good will, he had called on Mrs. Blakely and assured her that he would honor all the contracts her late husband had made for the band. Normally, partnership agreements were automatically discontinued by death and the surviving party was free from all obligations. But Sousa meant to be even better than fair toward Blakely's widow and daughter; he wanted to show them his most generous sympathy. He received no thanks.

The widow had a relative look after her interests, who tried to cut Sousa's basic salary by 100 dollars a week; made new dates which Sousa refused to accept; dismissed Christianer and hired someone else with whom Sousa refused to work. Then, charging breach of contract, the Blakely lawyers attempted to tie up Sousa's royalties and box-office receipts, informing publishers and local managers that he was not entitled to collect.

Sousa countered by threatening to stop the concert and

send the audience home, should his treasurer be prevented from collecting during the second number. It was embarrassing, unpleasant, undignified. In Waterbury, Connecticut, he had to get a lawyer in the middle of the night because a gushing young woman manager refused to produce the money. It turned out that the pert young lady had done so to demonstrate her executive ability because she wanted to become manager of Sousa's Band!

An astute lawyer once said that a good partnership was one in which neither party bothered to check the contract. And, he added wistfully, that, if they did so after the first difficulties arose, they would either find that its legal subtleties did not apply to their dispute or they would be sorry to have signed at all.

Both were true in Sousa's case. He did feel sorry that he had signed so hastily and carelessly, without trying for better terms. But even a better contract would hardly have altered the present situation.

He was ready to give credit where credit was due. What would have become of him without Blakely? An aging noncom whose talent would have withered from frustration. How would he have received publicity and stimulus for his compositions, if Blakely hadn't sent him trooping? His most successful works might have remained unwritten, and the rest wouldn't be selling half as well.

But Blakely hadn't done badly either. He had never printed any of Sousa's music as he had promised, yet collected half of the royalties. Neither of them had anticipated the amount of money they would be making for each other. That, technically, Sousa had been an employee of the Blakely Syndicate was an outdated absurdity that existed only on paper. He would not now stay in bondage to Blakely's heirs.

The Stars and Stripes broke the camel's back. Written after Blakely's death, but before expiration of the five-year contract, to which Sousa continued to adhere in other matters of his own free will, its royalties became an issue open to interpretation and dispute. And with the fantastic success of the march a small fortune was at stake.

Mrs. Ada Blakely went to court. As executrix of the estate she claimed one half of Sousa's earnings and title to the name of "Sousa's Band" which, she insisted, was a trade-mark her late husband had established and promoted.

Sousa hired a lawyer in Philadelphia to fight this fantastic claim to his money and his name. The lawyer argued that the money Blakely had collected had been tantamount to a manager's fees which did not have to be paid after services were discontinued. But the contractual implications were not so simple and the matter dragged on for several years.

Meantime, in 1900, Sousa's trip to Europe became a reality. Another Paris World's Fair was to open that summer, and for two years American bandleaders had been scrambling for engagements at the United States pavilion. Innes even hurried abroad as soon as preparations started, vainly hoping to return with a contract; Sousa's Band won the appointment as official musical representative of the U.S.A.

Naturally they did not expect to confine their activities to France. A European impresario offered to send them half across the Continent. But then, two weeks before they were to sail, the man dropped dead and this voided all arrangements he had made.

Sousa dispatched Colonel Hinton to recover some dates and make new contracts. But time was so short that Sousa could not possibly learn about the state of his European affairs until he arrived in England.

His New York manager was a youngish man, Everett B. Reynolds, whom he had met at Manhattan Beach. As a general assistant to Mr. Corbin, Reynolds had watched Sousa break all previous attendance records and then steadily better his own mark. When Corbin died, and Sousa had not yet found a successor to Blakely, Reynolds applied. He was not a rich man, but he could offer some financial backing and had a good business record. Sousa decided to try him. Especially if he took the band overseas, he did not want to assume all the responsibilities by himself.

Sousa returned to New York on April 22. He had only three days left before sailing, and plenty of work to do. But in his office he found a restive Reynolds, a changed man who abruptly demanded an extension of their contract to be drawn up and signed at once.

"Why, it runs for one more year. Can't it wait?" Sousa asked irritably.

Reynolds said it couldn't.

But Sousa was firm. He had to see how they would make out in Europe, he explained, before he could think of the future. Under the circumstances the tour might be the acid test of their collaboration. If successful, he would be foolish to let the contract expire. If unsuccessful, he would give Reynolds an opportunity to make up for his share in the deficit, but he could not and would not commit himself beyond that. It was the worse possible moment, he added impatiently, to press him for long-term arrangements.

But for Reynolds this seemed the only possible moment. And he did want to apply pressure.

Living in the hub of musical gossip, speculation, grapevine, and intrigue, he had come to wonder whether Europeans would like Sousa as well as they liked his marches. His appearance, his demeanor, the little oddities and mannerisms he had been cultivating lately, which Americans cherished, wouldn't they antagonize people abroad? Europeans might be stuffy, jealous of the foreigner, who could tell? Sousa was not the person to have a lukewarm reception; it would be either hit or miss.

Reynolds, however, did not want to just break even. He could not risk being jobless in another year, his professional reputation badly impaired, should Sousa fail abroad. He wanted a fair amount of security. He did not want his career to be at the mercy of Sousa's whims and moods, and of a foreign public's unpredictable reactions.

"Unless we get this settled, I'll have to withdraw from the trip," he ventured, confident that the pressure of time would swing Sousa's decision in his favor.

"As you wish." Sousa got up.

"But . . ." A startled Reynolds had no chance to retract. The office door closed.

Sousa's face was taut as he walked down Fifty-seventh Street. Such a stupid attempt at coercion!

Well, then, alone!

He stopped at his bank for two letters of credit, notified Reynolds that their agreement was terminated, and paid him off. He did not tell his men, and not even Jane, what had happened. When things went dangerously wrong, he preferred not to discuss them.

In Madison Square Garden he ran into John L. Sullivan. "I hear you're going to Europe?" the champion addressed him.

"Yes, we're going over and we hope to please them," Sousa replied with a hardly audible sigh.

"Please them! You'll knock the hell out of 'em!" This was a shot in the arm.

Jane and the girls accompanied him to the pier. They stood around chatting as, through luggage and people flitting past, Reynolds picked his way toward their group. Jane did not understand why Sousa hustled the other man away and why he seemed so tense and angry as he listened to his excited talk.

"And I am going to play all over Europe, six months, no matter what happens," they heard Sousa's raised voice and saw Reynolds trudge off like a beaten dog.

Sousa stood there, obviously thinking very hard, his brow deeply furrowed. Reynolds had come to dissuade him from going alone—from going altogether; but Sousa had lost confidence in him, whatever he now said.

"That man's got cold feet," he answered his wife's mute question. His face twitched but slightly. That was all.

The SS *St. Louis* blew its whistle. Late-comers scurried past. Sousa patted the girls' cheeks, kissed Jane, and strode up the gangplank in full composure, to embark on a journey involving 500,000 dollars and responsibility for 62 men, without manager, without backing, and without bookings outside his assignment at the Fair.

chapter eighteen

Colonel Hinton, who met them in Southampton, reported that things didn't look too bad after all. He had arranged concerts in practically every major town of Belgium, Holland, Germany. Sousa appointed him tour manager, and they left at once for Paris, for their first concert on May 5.

It was a splendid, balmy day. Paris, never lovelier than in the spring, was glittering with sunlight and blossoms. The air was heavy with sweet scents. The timing was perfect. The bewildering bustle of the opening of the Fair was over, but the novelty had not yet worn off. Foreigners were trooping in, and Parisians had not yet left for their long vacations. Days were charged with adventure and enchanting discovery.

The bandsmen were startled when they first inspected the locale between the Champs-Élysées and the Dome des Invalides where Napoleon lies buried. Old Paris itself provided the backdrop, ancient noble edifices, all marble steps, statues, trees and bushes, the whole animated by billows of flags. Between two sumptuous palaces housing part of the Exposition, Sousa was to start playing at 3:30 P.M. Two rows of chairs around an empty circle marked the place.

At 2:30 people started coming, and by 3 o'clock the

esplanade was jammed. A colorful crowd in street clothes or exotic costumes chattered in the oddest accents and idioms, as they waited for the arrival of "those Americans."

First to arrive were a truckload of American trunks, and a nice-looking young man in a nondescript uniform. People watched in amazement the strange prelude and paraphernalia of the show.

Without speaking and with only the sparsest of gestures, he supervised the speedy unloading, as another young man, in a different uniform, emerged as if from nowhere and proceeded to rearrange the chairs into a wider circle. Frenchmen given to effusive oratory and theatrical gesticulation for the most commonplace procedures, particularly if performed on the street, waited for the two to break out into dance steps or stylized pantomime. Yet, there was no unnecessary motion, no fumbling, not a moment's interruption. The men worked with clocklike precision, evidently following a carefully worked-out plan, and totally oblivious of spectators.

A huge square box was set up in front of one palace entrance. Young Man Number 1 lifted the lid: pieces of white and gold wood, bedded in folds of a cloth of glowing scarlet and held in place by stacks of black folios, shimmered in the sun. He removed the cloth, placed the heaviest piece of timber on the ground, screwed on a lighter one, fixed a flat one with an S chiseled into the center, on top at an angle, and placed a delicate white and gold baton on the completed conductor's desk. Simultaneously, Number 2 tackled another box containing bundles of iron rods which he untied and shook into position, one after another, until they turned into music stands which he placed in front of the chairs. Then, while Number 1 covered the flat box with the red cloth and made sure that it stood in line with the palace gate, Number 2 distributed the black folios beside the chairs and dropped small volumes looking like hymnbooks on the seats. The two men did not once cross each other's path, and did not utter a sound as they worked, the one on the conductor's, the other on the musicians', tools and props; they finished simultaneously and vanished out of sight. The audience was intrigued. Did Mr. Sousa give such a show to his Americans once or twice every day?

Gay sounds were heard in the distance; hurrahs and the clapping of hands gushed down the avenue. Down the sunlit esplanade marched the dark-clad bandsmen, like a black serpent gliding over a gaily patterned carpet. High precision was in their procession, yet nothing of the automatic briskness of European columns in motion; and as if to underline the absence of militaristic pretense, each man carried a newspaper under his arm. "Reading, always reading, those Americans," one of the crowd marveled, "that's what makes them so successful."

The column was spearheaded by two gigantic American flags which swung in acknowledgment of the applause. Smartly the men filed to their chairs, tossed their newspapers underneath, and readied their instruments. Glittering brass reflected distorted pictures of trees, clouds, and buildings.

Next, ten American guards walked up, white trimmings on their uniforms, young, tall, vigorous, handsome youths. But they looked drab in comparison to an eleventh who led them, a giant with a cherub's face, wearing a gilt-edged coat. Ladies of all ages and complexions held their breath.

Striding behind their leader, the guards marched around

the bandsmen, one after another falling out of formation until they stood in a circle behind Sousa's men. Into the circle moved the standard-bearers. They had gathered the folds of the Stars and Stripes and held them firmly in gloved hands. The gloves were immaculately white. "What clean and quiet men!" the French commented.

The clapping of hands resumed, exploded like a gun salute. Sousa had stepped out of the palace and descended the marble steps between waving flags—radiant, poised, saluting snappily as he reached the stand. The fit and finish of his uniform was superb; people noticed his custom-made high-heeled shoes, and his gloves so tight that only one button could be closed: Sousa wanted his hands to look as small as possible when conducting.

The small white-gloved hand raised the gilded baton. A roll of drums—banners dipped in salute—scattered voices rising: *Oh say, can you see* . . . Americans in the audience sang in patriotic nostalgia, as Sousa raised their anthem like a conquering flag.

His success was instantaneous and complete. People liked everything, his arrangements of new operas and old American folksongs, even of the *Marseillaise*. Strange as the setup was, the man on the podium spoke to them as an old acquaintance, for after every number came one of his marches to which almost everyone on the sunbaked plaza had danced or sung or laughed or cried some time in his life. The climax came with *The Stars and Stripes*. When the refrain came, the cornet players who carried the melody lined up in front; a huge American flag unfurled atop the stairs waved over the audience and saluted three times. An American ex-officer from Galesburg, Illinois, shed tears. A beturbaned Arab sat nodding the rhythm. A young Chinese beat time with his umbrella. Hats flew into the air, handkerchiefs fluttered, hurrahs broke into the final chord in unrestrained enthusiasm for America and her flag.

The first pinkish shadows of the declining day had appeared in the sky when the last visitors departed and indefatigable tourists proceeded to the Dome. The echoes of the *Marseillaise* and *The Stars and Stripes* still in their ears, they entered the galleries from where they could look down on Napoleon's onyx coffin surrounded by statues symbolizing the battles he had fought. Small bunches of violets withered on the sarcophagus: May 5 was also the anniversary of Napoleon's death. But few, if any, of the visitors knew about the startling prophecy the fallen emperor had made about the budding republic across the waters: "Watch out for America over there," Napoleon had said, "you shall need her one day!"

France had emerged from more than a century of upheavals, wars, glory, and disaster as one of the wealthiest nations in the world and in exuberant spirits. Wealth, the French were certain, would restore their country to its dominant role in world affairs. Already an alliance with Russia had been signed to keep Germany in the claws of a juggernaut, and billions of French savings went into Russian bonds, huge amounts of French supplies into the immense but ill-equipped armies of the same Russia that had entered Paris in 1814 as vanguards of the victorious allies. French industrial prowess, French riches, French pride and self-confidence were manifested at the Fair and in its attendance. Pent-up emotions waited to be released

147

and lavished on any exciting object, be it a national controversy or an international pageant.

As the pageant of the World's Fair opened, a tempestuous controversy kept sentiments at fever pitch. The revolting affair of Captain Alfred Dreyfus, which reverberated around the world, split France into two camps. Important military secrets had been sold to the German Military Attaché. Captain Dreyfus had been charged with the crime, court-martialed and found guilty, and exiled to the notorious penal colony of Devil's Island—an inconspicuous, bewildered prisoner who never rose to the emotional impact of his fate.

But the best minds of France insisted that he had been framed. Georges Clemenceau, later French Prime Minister; Émile Zola, the celebrated novelist; Maître Labori, giant of the bar, they all worked, spoke, wrote, for Dreyfus' rehabilitation. Dreyfusards and anti-Dreyfusards crusaded against each other in parlors and pubs; newspapers featured Dreyfus; the Chamber carried the issue into every debate; the French Academy talked Dreyfus in lofty terms; the mob shouted the Alsatian name, so difficult to pronounce, as a battlecry. Dreyfus ignited nationalistic explosives and unleashed tempests of chauvinism. Only after five years of detention would Dreyfus be acquitted, promoted, and decorated; his accuser—the real culprit—committed suicide.

No foreigner could fail to know about the case, but to many the rage in Paris must have had a touch of extravagance, if not lunacy. Sousa's orderly mind could not conceive of justice shaped in tumult. He observed with keen interest the strange workings of Gallic tempers. Those who had shouted themselves hoarse in ugly arguments could almost without transition, divert their passions to a march or, say, to a band arrangement of selections from Puccini's newest opera, *La Bohème*.

Every afternoon during the two weeks that Sousa's band played, the esplanade was packed with human beings wedged into a solid block, with nobody even attempting to circulate.

Sousa became the Pied Piper of Paris. Crowds, growing like avalanches, followed him on his strolls. A distant cousin who lived in the French capital once saw a multi-colored wave of humanity roll up an avenue, and as it came closer he noticed that it followed in the wake of his famous relative. The gay mass floated toward a corner where an old woman stood grinding a barrel organ; the pathetic emptiness of a metal plate on the pavement in front of her, told a story of desperation. "Hold your apron up!" Sousa said as he gently pushed the woman aside and seized the crank. She obeyed and stood, stiff and bewildered, her apron unfolded, as Sousa cranked with verve and gusto, his free hand pointing at the beggar. People laughed and cheered, pressed nearer; coins flitted through the air, started to come in torrents, tinkled in the woman's apron until it was filled to overflowing. Sousa stopped cranking, bowed to the woman, hand on his heart, said something pleasant in broken French no one could fully understand, waved to his spectators, and walked away with twinkling eyes and a light heart, well satisfied with everybody.

He had not expected such temperamental reaction in foreign lands, so intense a personal popularity bursting forth at the slightest provocation. Everybody loved him and he loved everybody. On May 15, when he marched his band past the German Exposition Building as the dedicatory ceremonies were under way, he decided to serenade the coexhibitors; but the German national anthem having the same melody as the British, he had the band strike up *Die Wacht am Rhein*. This was about as harmless as sticking a burning torch into a tubful of gunpowder. *Die Wacht am Rhein* had been the theme song of the Franco-Prussian War. To Frenchmen in their fifties who had seen action, it was a reminder of past disgrace, an insult without parallel; and even to the younger generation it was salt rubbed into wounds. Since then, World's Fairs had been championing peace and commerce between France and her hereditary enemy, but they could not commandeer love. No German would have dared to play the tune. An alarmed official tried to stop Sousa, who, however, failed to see why a free American should not pay his courtesies in whatever manner he chose. Had only one Frenchman hissed, a major international incident might have developed. But no one ever hissed Sousa.

The story of the American who had played *Die Wacht am Rhein* in the heart of France traveled quickly through the Reich, ahead of the band which, after concerts in Brussels and Liége, came to Germany. The first week was spent in Berlin, the second in the big port city of Hamburg. Then followed Bremen, another ancient naval town; industrial Hanover and Dresden; romantic Ulm on the Danube; Frankfort, site of the French-German peace conference of 1871; Cologne-on the-Rhine. Finally, after a tour of Bavaria, they were scheduled to return to Paris, to start the second part of their engagement on Independence Day.

Every concert was crowded to capacity. Kroll's Garden in Berlin counted 16,000 one day. In Dresden the road leading uphill to the Bergkeller, where they played, was densely lined with people every afternoon. Saxonian socialites waved down from the balconies in this swank neighborhood. *The Washington Post* was just as popular in Europe then as it had been ten years before in America. And as Sousa and his band swept through part of the Continent, they blanketed it with ragtime, two-steps, old Negro melodies.

Sousa's personal habits were watched with the same curiosity as, ordinarily, the refined eccentricities of foreign potentates. No other band traveled by special train; the press commented on the Sousa train so elaborately that nobody on its route could fail to learn the precise time of its arrival. Observers wondered about these musicians who carried all they needed in two pieces of luggage per man, but dragged the conductor's podium around. And then, instead of keeping their delicate musicians' hands off rough activities, they would don sports outfits with "Sousa" written in big characters across the blouses, and troop to some ball field, where the reed would play against the brasses. Soccer addicts wondered about the strange game in which the ball was hit with a bat instead of foot or head, and they were amazed at *Herr* Sousa, who would appear on the field in full sports regalia and ceremoniously toss the first ball. Europeans decided that he was a man of surprises, at least as colorful and interesting as, say, visiting royalty from Persia or Montenegro.

No other bandmaster traveled with such pomp and circumstance. No other threw such lavish parties at his hotel. And no European bandleader used saxophones, for that matter; no other had ever thought of placing the trombones in front of the platform; no other made his transcription in the original keys to keep them as close as possible to the orchestral versions, for no other band had players with such superb technique. And if the *Berliner Morgenpost,* the morning paper with the largest circulation in Germany, hailed Sousa as the "Johann Strauss of the New World," his ace soloist Arthur Pryor acquired the epithet of "Paganini of the slide trombone."

Searching minds undertook to analyze the elements of Sousa's success. Some thought that it was the variety of his programs, the obvious determination to play only music which held audience interest, never merely because it was new or difficult. Others said that it was his elegant appearance, and still others admired the nonchalance of his conducting, which seemed to intimate that the most difficult pieces were easy for his band.

Wherever Sousa played outdoors, he made sure that there was plenty of space between band and spectators before the concert started; for, invariably, at the first encore, people would get up from their seats and press forward in order to miss nothing of his peculiar manner of acting out his music. This well-planned setting always brought the same spontaneous reaction. The magnet that attracted Americans exerted its force just as strongly abroad.

"He acts as if exhibiting tamed dogs or monkeys; then again he behaves like a Prussian general, and then again he doesn't conduct at all," the foreign correspondent of the *Pester Lloyd* wrote.

"He wields his baton like a whip, then again like an egg beater," a Belgian paper said.

"At times he seems to hold in his left hand the reins of [horses], in his right hand a whip; at times his head bends toward his shoulder, apparently aiming, gun in hand, at the brass drum. He swims, he dances, he fences—everything in harmony with the music," the Berlin *Die Welt am Montag* marveled.

All this was a far cry from the soldierly staidness of Sousa's conducting of only several years before. It did not always please those whom it puzzled. Some actually laughed at it, and jealousy had a plausible case. Deriders did not realize that Sousa's antics were artificial only in part, but mainly manifestations of temperament, of his own pleasure at shaping sounds, of his personal captivation by the swing of the music. He was "entering heart and soul into the life of a piece," he might explain. And when he conducted the alluring, passionate music of Spain, Italy, Hungary, he felt his hot Southern blood pulsating through his veins and was incapable of repressing his movements. But very rarely, if ever, did his play-acting deceive people about his real stature as a musician, about the discipline of his men, the up-to-dateness of his programs, the fecundity of his melodic invention, his daring use of modern effects. "Such marches! Such gladness and clamor and jubilation!" exulted the staid Amsterdam *Echo*. "These are marches to lead one, marching, to the end of the earth."

"Jupiter disorganized the elements, Sousa has disciplined them," wrote a newspaper in Belgium where Sousa was awarded the Cross of Artistic Merit, First Class, of the Academy in Hainault.

They returned to Paris on July 3 and next morning played at the dedication of the statues of George Washington and Lafayette. A new march, *The Man Behind the Gun*, added splendor to the occasion. After the ceremonies Sousa's Band paraded through the boulevards to a reception at the American Embassy. A picturesque detail of the Guarde Republicaine and American Guards escorted the band, stopping the always-chaotic traffic on the thoroughfares. In the afternoon of the eventful day they gave their regular concert on the Exposition grounds, and in the evening they played for three solid hours on the Place de l'Opéra. Again traffic had to be halted. The coachmen of Paris, notorious for their colorful vocabulary of discontent and for its profuse application against anybody interfering with their antics, did not protest. Until one o'clock in the morning, 40,000 people listened to French and American music, and they applauded heartily when a deputation of American residents presented their illustrious countryman with a huge American flag.

Shortly after Sousa left Paris, something happened which both amused and annoyed him and made much noise in France. Asked by a *Herald* correspondent about his impressions of music in Europe, he had seized the opportunity to start with a subject very close to his heart: government subsidy.

"An artistic organization that is fostered by state aid is like a hardy plant brought up in a hothouse," he said. "It may keep on living [but] it will always be sickly."

Although as a struggling young man he had rather favored the idea, he admitted, he had been "converted completely by a comparison of the superior results produced by individual effort with those due to a governmentally subsidized art."

In Europe subsidies were handed out freely; they were the basis of the musical setup in all major countries; but the concerts Sousa had heard in France and Germany did not cause him to amend his views. He had found most bands excellent, but excellent either in concert or on parade, not sufficiently adaptable to a change of settings. And he had been appalled by European program policy which he considered ultranationalistic. In nine symphony concerts he had heard in Paris, for example, only a handful out of some 60 numbers had been non-French. This, also, he attributed to "the evil influence of governmental support, which always creates a tendency to work in a groove, to stop in a rut."

It was convenient, too convenient, to play native music on public funds. Government-sponsored security, coupled with artistic regimentation, killed ambition and the competitive spirit, eliminated the necessity to please. "If a musician, a writer, a painter, has anything in him, he will dig it out of himself, if the state will only let him starve long enough," he went on. And later: "[Among] musicians, conductors, and composers . . . those who are most famous, most popular with the people, and whose reputation has passed the frontiers of their respective countries, are precisely those who have been left untrammeled by government or official bonds and who have been compelled to put forward the best that was in them by the beneficent law of the survival of the fittest."

A few days after the lengthy interview appeared, a man who signed himself "Musician" and claimed to be an American sent an open letter to the *Herald,* taking exception to Sousa's statements. The writer charged the bandleader with chauvinism and preposterous haughtiness toward the old continent, and glumly predicted that his celebrated compatriot was harming rather than furthering American prestige and transatlantic relations.

When the letter was printed Sousa was in Germany, on

the last leg of his trip which was to wind up in Amsterdam, Holland, on August 26. He minced no words in his reply, attacking his critic with the most effective weapon—ridicule. He restated with dignity that, in his opinion, French bands would be even better, and the French nation richer of Massenets, Bizets, Berliozes, if more musicians would "escape government appropriations" and "went forth into God's sunlight of freedom . . ." And he made it plain that, despite having enjoyed European hospitality, he did not renounce his right to criticize "a system that [he] believe[d] detrimental to the best interest of art."

Sousa's original remarks had nearly gone unnoticed. But after the two Americans started their polemics, French editorial writers took up the matter with gusto and built it into a "case," a controversy of the kind that culture-conscious Parisians always have relished and always will.

It seems that Sousa had not fully understood the mechanics of European state sponsorship, which had originated in many courts, large and small, vying for cultural accomplishment, and had far fewer strings attached than under a system in which modern partisan politics would determine appropriations. Also, he did not realize that the musical nationalism he had noticed was just another manifestation of the general nationalism rampant practically all over the world.

When the SS *St. Louis* steamed into New York harbor on September 19, Sousa's Band was on the forward deck playing *Home Sweet Home*. Sousa checked into the Netherlands Hotel and met the press. The tour that had discouraged his manager had turned into a bonanza.

"And it convinced me," he said, "that the world over human nature is the same, that there are certain elemental forces common to all enlightened people. The stolid German, the deliberate Dutchman, the fiery Frenchman, are all susceptible to the same melodic influences, are all stirred by the same kind of music that arouses American audiences to enthusiasm."

Affections must not be limited by puzzling boundary lines crisscrossing a small continent full of nice people; and at his comeback concert at the Metropolitan Opera House, he had the American, French, and German flags planted on the stage in a brotherly file.

chapter nineteen

I N OCTOBER, 1900, the Supreme Court of Pennsylvania rendered the final decision in the Blakely case. Sousa was traveling when he learned of the verdict. The estate was to get Blakely's contractual share from Sousa's works written before November, 1896, and from publishers' agreements entered before May 23, 1897. The court ruled that all the compositions Sousa had written while under contract had been common property of himself and Blakely, his "employer."

However, and most important, Sousa retained full control of the name of his band.

This was a great relief to him, for the idea that his name might have become a "trade-mark" belonging to Blakely had worried him no end. A different court decision might have enabled Mrs. Ada Blakely to form a "New Sousa Band" or the like without ever consulting him, or make him a tributary to the estate and dependent on its whims, unless he wanted to pay an exorbitant fee for the use of his own name. It would have been absurd, but the possibility could not be ruled out until the litigation had come to an end.

Under those circumstances the large cuts from his income which would be going to the estate annoyed him less than might have been expected. He decided to write this off and discuss it as little as possible.

The band's fifth transcontinental tour, which followed the European without a breathing spell, was like a triumphant procession. Sousa was the first native musician who had traveled so extensively abroad; he was the entire country's local-boy-who-had-made-good.

A Pennsylvanian trudged over 40 miles of rugged mountains to see the man who was making 25,000 dollars a year on his compositions alone. In Olympia, Washington, the state legislature could transact no business on the afternoon of a Sousa matinee because the majority of both houses sat in the concert; a messenger dispatched to round up a quorum ended up by staying himself. Sousa was still touring in the spring when he was informed that the French government had awarded him the palms of the Academy, in recognition of his outstanding achievements while in France.

His main engagements that year were three expositions: Buffalo, Pittsburgh, and Glasgow, Scotland.

Buffalo was a big Pan-American affair, rousingly successful; Sousa's march *Invincible Eagle* commemorates the event. He had already left when the inspiring spectacle turned into tragedy: for it was at this exposition that an anarchist's gun fatally wounded President McKinley who had come to Buffalo to meet notables from abroad.

The appearance of Sousa's Band in Glasgow had been booked the previous year, and he considered it a welcome opportunity for another transatlantic voyage. An extended tour through England, which included 15 concerts in London alone, was to follow. This time Jane accompanied him.

They arrived in London on the morning of October 4. A few hours later at a stag luncheon given in his honor, Sousa startled a distinguished committee which included a Member of Parliament, several aristocrats, and Mr. George Ashton, in charge of Court entertainment, by the dead-pan humor of his improvised speech. Managing to squeeze three Albert Hall concerts into his first two days on British soil, he played to a total of 27,000 enthusiastic Londoners; it seems that, considerate of a public with a conservative reputation, Sousa was careful to eliminate the purely visual attractions of his conducting, for one critic spoke of his striking modesty and self-suppression.

In Glasgow, after four spectacularly successful weeks, their farewell concert boosted the Fair's turnstile count to 152,709, the second largest for a single day.

Back in London, animated hours were spent in the company of Lieutenant Dan Godfrey, one of three bandmaster brothers, and leader of the famed Royal Grenadiers. The Grenadiers had been the only other band at Glasgow, and

159

initial rivalries had been highly unpleasant, but Sousa's diplomatic skill turned a potential enemy into a devoted friend. Eventually Godfrey arranged Strauss' *Till Eulenspiegel* for Sousa's Band and helped Sousa on his perennial search of new repertory works. "It will rejoice my young and tender soul if you will have handy for me to look over such scores as you think will adapt themselves to effective instrumentation for my justly celebrated band," Sousa once wrote to him.

That first season in London the justly celebrated March King was lionized by the smart set. Albert de Rothschild gave the Sousas a party at which Melba sang and Ysaye played. Then, early in December, Mr. Ashton came to the hotel and asked to talk with Sousa, absolutely alone.

After the valet had left the room, Mr. Ashton explained in a hushed voice that King Edward desired a command performance at Sandringham Castle the next Sunday, but wished the matter to be kept in strict secrecy; the occasion was the Queen's birthday, and the concert was to be a surprise for her.

Sousa deliberated for a moment, then asked and obtained permission to take two persons into his confidence: Mrs. Sousa, who must be appropriately dressed for presentation at Court, and Baron Rothschild, who would have to help if there should be no leak.

While Colonel Hinton bombarded the London press with news items that Sousa's Band would be giving a concert at the Rothschild country place on Sunday, Jane sat in session with a Parisian designer named Beer. But when the 500-dollar dress, all ice-blue taffeta and velvet ribbons, was delivered, Sousa decided that the color was too cold for the occasion and picked a gown of heavy white silk dotted with pink roses from his wife's wardrobe.

Not until after their train pulled out did the bandsmen learn their real destination. To play for the King and Queen of England was a treat, a thrill; the men cheered and enjoyed themselves like boys throughout the four-hour trip to Wolferton, the station for Sandringham.

An array of soft-cushioned royal carriages waited for them. The Sousas rode in the King's private automobile. In the opaque darkness they could not see much of the landscape, but the castle itself was resplendent with light. As they were led upstairs, Jane noticed how beautiful simplicity could be. There was no touch of oppressive pompousness in the King's summer palace; it was a country squire's home, solid, comfortable, good to live in.

At 10:30 sharp, Sousa's Band entered the ballroom that had been converted into a concert hall. About 20 persons were present: the royal family and their house guests in the front row, and behind them several neighbors and tenants. At the King's request, Sousa's program contained many of his marches. Hardly ever had the band played with greater sparkle and verve. It was a grand concert on a grand occasion. *The Star-Spangled Banner* had to be repeated four times, and the Queen demanded to hear *Nearer My God to Thee*—a gesture to the memory of President McKinley whose favorite tune it had been.

The King seemed well pleased with the concert and with the surprise he had given his wife on her first birthday as a Queen. He had just turned 60 when he ascended the throne, *bon-vivant* son of a mother whose very name has enriched the vocabulary with a new word for decorous modesty. Queen Victoria had not been amused by her son's generosity as a patron of Parisian *boîtes de nuit*, which had been a topic of debate in the Commons; and politicians on both sides of the House had feared that the pleasure-loving Prince might be lacking in statesmanship, only to find later that he made a clever and dignified King.

Edward VII liked sports and music. One of his horses had just won the Grand National and he never missed a successful operetta. Sir Arthur Sullivan, for years his partner in clandestine Sunday night poker sessions, was dead, and hardly any other artist could replace him in the King's affections; but Edward liked the good-looking Americans, their natural poise, their sprightly music.

"Your marches are like your people," the Queen said to Sousa. "Full of fire, brilliance, and sentiment."

The King praised *El Capitan* which he had seen.

Then he beckoned to an equerry who brought a small box in which a silver medal lay on soft velvet. "I hope you will accept this in remembrance of the pleasant occasion and as a recognition of your services to one of the most delightful of the arts."

It was the Victorian Order, designed by the late Queen, the highest medal the British Commonwealth would bestow upon an artist. Sousa knew of no other American who had yet received it, and of no other musician except Jean de Reszke.

The box in his hands, he looked at his wife. Her eyes shone and her cheeks had flushed the color of the roses on her dress. The golden overtones in the shining whiteness of her hair reflected the sparkle of the candelabra. She looked every bit as noble as the ladies of the Court.

The Queen followed his eyes. "Mrs. Sousa is very beautiful," she said and smiled. Sousa thought so himself.

A stately march melody rose in him as vividly as if he had written it long ago. "I have a fine idea," he turned to the King. "The melody for a march just came to me. I hope Your Majesty will grant permission to dedicate it to you."

The King assured him that he would be delighted. The Prince of Wales took the box from Sousa's hand. "Where do you want me to pin it?" he asked, lifting the medal from its cushion.

"Over my heart . . ."

"How verrry American!"

Sousa went to Europe four more times within the next few years. The *Imperial Edward* march was graciously accepted and transposed to suit England's major military bands. In 1903 he conducted again at the Queen's birthday party, gave another command performance at Windsor Castle, and was rewarded by a gift of four pheasants the King had shot himself. Once after a concert he was the King's supper guest, with his host and himself swapping sports stories until the small hours. Sousa was in his element as he described hunting in America—the adventures of the Wild West and the delights of the desert; anecdotes about quail, deer, and horses; his campfire conversations with cowboys and mountaineers. Of all the countries he visited, Sousa always liked England best.

He did not rest on his laurels when at home. On tour he still gave two concerts daily, for otherwise not even a packed house would have made the band a paying proposition. Their itinerary included 240 towns in an average year.

His friends agreed that he was thriving on pressure.

They marveled at his capacity for work, for concentration, for new pursuits.

In 1902 Sousa turned novelist. A plot he had long had in mind—dealing with a soul-searching violinist, his unhappy love, a beautifully sounding instrument given to him by Satan, and the irresistible urge to play on its forbidden string of death—turned into a 125-page novelette written in a style that seems awkward and circumstantial even for Sousa's day. Originally Sousa had discussed the story with Mr. Bok of *The Saturday Evening Post* and offered it to the magazine for 5000 dollars. But he disliked the idea of having to submit the finished manuscript like an ordinary author, and instead of sending it to Philadelphia he put it in his trunk. *The Fifth String* went on tour with Sousa's Band as far as Indianapolis, where it was sold across the banquet table to Mr. Bobbs, head of the Bobbs-Merrill Company, publishers. Carried by the March King's name and the novelty of his endeavor, the book climbed to near the top of the best-selling list and stayed there for a considerable length of time. This achievement made Sousa even prouder than his musical successes, which he had come to take for granted. A sale of 55,000 copies was not bad, as a first try by an author nearing 50.

Three years later his second book followed, *Pipetown Sandy*, a semiautobiographical juvenile in which he reminisced about his childhood in a casual style interspersed with slang and Gilbertian verse. Now he could talk about "my novels" and never missed an opportunity of doing so.

In 1905 the band concertized its way from London, via France, Belgium, and Germany, to St. Petersburg, where it opened a series of nine performances on Tsar Nicholas' birthday, May 16. Sousa was appalled by regimentation in Russia. It was the only country in Europe one could not visit without a passport, and also he had to submit in advance the precise texts of all their advertisements, programs, and songs. The latter was particularly annoying, since his soprano soloist Estelle Liebling not only sang in half a dozen different languages but also had a number of coloratura pieces on her program, which consisted largely of vocalization. And because not even Sousa dared wire a Russian censor that some vocal pieces would be sung to "Ah-ah-ah," Miss Liebling agreed to use the texts of *Annie Rooney* and *Marguerite* for all the songs and arias on the bill.

Russia was just losing the war with Japan which had opened more than one year before with a Japanese sneak attack on the Russian fleet, and had already led to the loss of Port Arthur and subsequently to a series of Russian debacles at that naval fortress, and all the way from Northern Korea, via the Yalu River, to Mukden. Since France was the ally of Russia, England Japan's close friend, and Germany the organizer of the Japanese Army, the United States was the most logical mediator. President Theodore Roosevelt was already closely watching developments. In those days of tension the police were even more on the alert than usual, and even as harmless and congenial a group as an American concert band was under constant surveillance.

Sousa's audience in St. Petersburg's Cisnelli Circus consisted almost entirely of officers and officials and their ladies. Very few other people were present. The royal box was draped so that nobody could tell whether the Tsar and his family attended, but Sousa had reason to assume that they did. He had been requested to open the concert with the Russian national anthem, and to repeat it as often as it met with a demonstration. As a typical American he promised to repeat it as often as the majority would applaud. He had to repeat it four times. Unrest exploded into patriotic demonstrations that paled all that Sousa had ever experienced before.

During intermission he was asked to start the second part with *The Star-Spangled Banner*. A functionary explained to the audience words and meaning of the anthem. At the drum roll everybody rose, and the men, almost all of them in uniform, stood at attention through several repetitions of the American national hymn.

After St. Petersburg came Warsaw (then still Russia), where Sousa found a hotel equipped with American comforts. It had been built by Paderewski, who had obviously imitated the finest and latest comforts he had seen on his American concert tours. As a farewell gift from Warsaw, he was presented with a long list of deductions from his earnings, including "police tax" as a major item. His stormy protest was heard by Jean de Reszke, who happened to be backstage with him and soothed Sousa by suggesting that he had better pay up, for this was definitely not America. Sousa never went back to Russia.

Next on their itinerary was Vienna, where they were booked for eight concerts in Venedig in Wien, an amusement park within the world-famous Prater, which catered to gay gentlemen from out of town and other seekers of summer entertainment. In Vienna, Sousa met a familiar American face: the former Countess Pourtallis who had gone to school with his sister Tinnie, and later married the Viennese operetta composer Emil Lindau whose *Frühlingsluft* was the current hit. At dinner they talked about the Strauss family. Johann had died six years ago. But Eduard was still around, a fading yet still handsome dandy, whose top hat and yellow gloves were landmarks of fashionable promenades; a disappointed, bitter man who spent his days attending Strauss memorials and fretting over insufficient attention. Aboard the steamer that had carried them back from a last American tour, Eduard had disbanded the orchestra that his father had founded and that his great brother had led to fame. This had been early in 1900, several months after the Waltz King's death and, by odd coincidence, shortly before another eastbound steamer took Sousa and his men abroad for the first time.

"Is the *Blue Danube* still popular here?" Sousa asked Lindau.

"Mr. Sousa, the *Blue Danube* will last as long as Vienna exists!"

And that night Sousa's Band sent the floating rhythm of the waltz rising to the crowns of the blooming old chestnut trees, and into its echoes blended the surging stride of *The Stars and Stripes*—the two most characteristic musical symbols that any two countries ever produced.

Touring orchestras usually played little, if any, music of the country they visited. Anxious to display the creative output of their own compatriots, they refrained from what might have been considered a presumptuous or naïve effort of carrying coals to Newcastle. Sousa, however, thought it a fitting courtesy to play not only the country's national anthem but also at least one composition by a local musical hero. As he played Strauss and Schubert in Vienna, he played Dvořák in Prague and Wagner in Saxony—and reaped flattering comments from public and press.

Hamburg, Denmark, Holland, England again; all the way through Europe, from the Atlantic to the fringe of Asia, and back, Sousa's Band was giving audiences a new notion of America. To the average European, America was the country where Caruso went and whence Houdini came; where Buffalo Bill performed his antics in the Wild West; where Theodore Roosevelt had done some "rough riding" before he became President, and later had spent 40 million dollars to acquire the uncompleted Panama Canal from the French; from where the Nick Carter adventure stories came; and where, according to a best-selling Saxonian author Carl May, Indians, trappers, and other armed men were performing exploits of which all European teen-age boys (including one Adolf Hitler of Upper Austria province) were dreaming. And now a bandful of American musicians had appeared in the flesh, led by a man who was the American success story personified: the baker's apprentice who had never finished school and yet had become a world celebrity in a medal-bedecked uniform.

Not all the spicy ingredients of the Sousa treat pleased everybody, however. Some said that Sousa courted the limelight, stooped to conquer, responded too quickly to the demand for encores. Some made fun of his mannerisms. In Francis Joseph's ornate Vienna, the unmilitaristic parading of the men in semimilitaristic garb drew indulgent smiles. Even in Sousa's favorite England there were dissenting voices: his brass was too loud, his new symphonic poem *At the King's Court* trite, his rendition of the *Tannhäuser* Overture lacking in climaxes. A London magazine writer opined that England had good players of her own and did not require transatlantic aid; and from 6000 miles west a San Franciscan echoed that Mr. Sousa was making a fool of himself and, by implication, of the United States.

Occasionally Sousa hit back at an unsympathetic critic, but he minded attack less than neglect. He scanned the papers every morning and if a concert went unmentioned his day was spoiled.

There were now gray hairs in his beard. There were acute attacks of illness or protracted periods of overexhaustion, when one of the bandsmen had to replace him at the stand. He no longer made his own band arrangements, but he did not employ a ghost writer for his compositions, even though rumors to that effect were spread by envious detractors.

There were also rumors of retirement; and every once in a while there was a "last concert," inevitably followed by a glorious comeback. Every tour was more successful than the previous one had been. Every time he returned from abroad people found that the band had never been so brilliant, Sousa's stock never so high.

One of his daughters still remembers a tour on which they left the train at Rocks Cliff, Wyoming, in the heart of the mining country. Rocks Cliff consisted of a railroad platform, a cluster of houses, and an auditorium; it looked as if no more than ten people could be drummed up in the entire village.

"How can you give a concert in a place like this?" she asked.

"You'll see," was Sousa's cryptic reply.

Long before concert time an audience started to arrive:

miners and their families, many still in working clothes, came from a radius of 100 miles to hear Sousa. Muddy boots stamped the rhythm; untrained voices sang with the music everybody seemed to know by heart.

Sousa had ceased to go to Manhattan Beach; the public had changed and the place was no longer to his liking. Since 1901 his main summer engagement was Willow Grove Park, ten miles from Philadelphia, one of those amusement parks that sprouted at the turn of the century, sponsored by the new streetcar lines to boost transportation. Willow Grove was far more than an amusement park, however. The Philadelphia Transportation Company turned it into "the summer music center of the world." At a time when summer festivals were few and far between, its huge extensible auditorium afforded many millions each summer an opportunity of hearing, free of charge, the best bands in America and even symphony orchestras like Damrosch's New Yorkers. Sousa remained a steady feature in Willow Grove for a quarter of a century.

To his men, Sousa was "The Governor," at times remote, then again very friendly. It was unthinkable to address him first, but occasionally he would single out a man and discuss with him horses, baseball, politics, music, even business, as they walked on a deck or stretched their legs on a station platform. At home they traveled in two special cars coupled to scheduled trains. Unless Sousa had a private compartment, he sat in the center near the aisle, notepaper always on his lap as he scribbled away. Sometimes he got up and wandered from man to man, invariably made a slight bow, said a few words, and walked away, but never started a real conversation.

To his many duties was added that of chaperone. It was

a responsibility to have two attractive women musicians travel with some 60 men, even though Jane, Priscilla or Helen, or all of them, came along frequently, and there were always several bandsmen's wives. Once a couple stayed with the band throughout an entire trip to be with their teen-age coloratura daughter. They need not have worried. Sousa's attitude toward his ladies was a mixture of Victorian paternalism and Latin chivalry; and, besides, a tour with Sousa became known as the best way to find a husband. "See that Sousa takes you on tour and you'll get married," was frequent advice to struggling young lady singers or violinists. Sousa saw it happen more than once: At some small station a young man turned up, greeted one of the young soloists with exclamations of surprise, carried her suitcase, sat in the auditorium, and vanished, only to reappear at the next stop. Sousa figured out that he could allow four repetitions of such "lucky surprises" before looking for a replacement.

How the girls ever managed to meet their men remains a riddle, however, as they were guarded like daughters of Spanish grandees. They were not supposed to mix with the bandsmen in off hours. While the men formed groups for sight-seeing when abroad, and boarded with local people to learn foreign customs, the girls had to stay with the Sousas in some pompous hotel, take their walks with the Sousas, eat with the Sousas in the dining room or, even worse, in the private suite, and The Governor, in person, knocked at their doors to fetch them for their meals. Sousa had little interest in museums, castles, and cathedrals but preferred long walks in the surrounding country; and the girls, in the long skirts of the early 1900's, had trouble keeping pace with his athletic stride. Once a young violinist

171

managed to sneak away to an amusement park. Riding on a merry-go-round—skirt flying, elaborate headgear dangerously slipping to one side, she suddenly sensed a stare and noticed The Governor watching her, quietly, hands on his hips. When he caught her eyes he shook his head and walked away. She was miserable when she returned to the hotel, and even more miserable when he did not mention the incident at all.

Sousa never scolded his musicians. He expected them to accept whatever necessary regulations he had to impose, and, well aware of the strain of their itinerant lives, he knew how much he could condone. "The Governor must have had some sixth sense," ex-bandsman Dr. Peter Buys recently reminisced in the *International Musician*, "that of selecting not only good musicians but men who would develop into regular troopers, men who could take the hardships of the road as a matter of course, and come up smiling."

A tour with Sousa meant permanent rushing: rushing from train to concert, from concert to hotel, or back to train. It meant sleeping in a different bed every night, or perhaps sitting up in the lobby of a Y or railroad station, if the management had not succeeded in securing accommodations in some small town. It might mean playing encores until after midnight and getting up at dawn to catch the train to their next matinee town. It meant performing the same two programs week after week, month after month. Sometimes the atmosphere got tense, tempers got short, the men got on each other's nerves, and the music began to bore them. Mistakes crept in, but Sousa would wait sardonically until the bandsmen corrected their own sour notes.

On one tour a man played F instead of F sharp persistently in the same passage through 35 concerts. Sousa looked at him expectantly every time the note came, but with no effect. Finally, when the other men began to grin and The Governor's stare grew ever more sarcastic, the culprit checked his part more closely, discovered his blunder, and corrected it. Sousa blew him a kiss, looked up at the ceiling, and took a deep breath of relief. This was his humorous form of reprimand.

But when a man took too long discovering an error, Sousa got very angry. He had a favorite invective—so strong that loyal bandsmen even now refuse to quote it—which he hissed at the band before turning around for an amiable bow to the audience. It was not addressed at anyone in particular but, as one old-timer put it, "it covered the entire band with a frosting of ice."

Sousa also used it when some player flirted too conspicuously with a girl in the audience. As, occasionally, singers do not know what to do with their hands, the men, who knew every note by heart, did not know what to do with their eyes. Since they did not have to look at the music and could not keep staring at the conductor for many hours every day, they let their eyes roam the auditorium and eventually would find some local belle to play to. "Don't believe he doesn't notice," older bandsmen might warn, "there isn't anything he doesn't see." Sousa would tolerate a certain amount of harmless fun; however, he could not chance the reputation of his band.

Sometimes tensions found vent in practical jokes. There was a German solo player, sensitive of stomach and soul, who distrusted food conditions on the road and carried his own sausages in his luggage. Once some of the boys ganged up and stole the man's whole supply; but after the first number, when he had been out front playing a solo on an empty stomach, he found the string of sausages attractively draped around his music stand. The man was virtually in tears when he appeared in the greenroom after the concert and complained to Sousa about the wickedness of the world. Sousa's eyes narrowed to a twinkle, but he could not afford to have his solo players upset. Next morning on the train, after some investigation, he had ringleader Emil Mix summoned into his private compartment. Mix stayed one hour, two hours, three, four. His accomplices grew apprehensive. After four and a half hours the tuba player emerged, smiling and exhausted. Sousa had talked baseball. The Governor had been at his most talkative and charming. For over four hours Mix had been on tenterhooks, standing by the door of the small, smoke-filled compartment, waiting for the storm to break: such was Sousa's way of disciplining members for minor offenses.

But there were instances—very rare exceptions—in which his face grew a bluish red, his voice rose to a roar, and he trembled with rage. Once, on a train, he seized a man by the collar and shook him so violently that other bandsmen had to intervene. At a small village station, hours away from the next town, the man was paid and put off the train. He was one of the most valuable players and irreplaceable on the road, but Sousa could stand his face no longer: the man had made a nasty remark about a lady soloist . . .

chapter twenty

I and those of you who want to join me, shall be gone for about a year," Sousa addressed his men early in 1910. "We shall play in all the chief cities of the world, and wherever else we are wanted. I shall pay you one third of your salaries while on shipboard, and a bonus —*if* we make a profit. But I can promise you nothing except the ordinary comforts of life on land and on sea. Those who want to come along will raise their hands."

Fifty-three hands rose in unison. No one wanted to stay behind.

Posters nine by 21 feet advertised the forthcoming world tour of "Sousa's Unrivaled Band." Telegraph wires hummed, typewriters clicked. It was a tremendous undertaking, requiring an enormous amount of work.

Sousa was again out to break new ground. It was no longer unusual for American artists to tour in Europe; a virtual invasion by American showpeople was hitting England. The time had come when American artists needed European successes to make good at home, and those who could not go boosted their prestige by plastering their luggage with fake stickers and labels of European hotels with which budding racketeers did a thriving business. But Sousa, who had conquered Europe when practically no one else had gone there, now wanted to conquer the world.

He wanted to play for men and women who might never have seen a genuine American. To take about threescore people, including ladies, through the Seven Seas was the greatest venture ever undertaken by an American musical organization.

Sousa's business manager then was Edwin L. Clarke, the cornetist's brother. Herbert Clarke doubled as Sousa's assistant; trombonist Mark Lyons as baggage master; tympanist Dr. Willie Lowe as physician. The Quinlan Agency booked the tour from London. As it took shape Sousa was impressed with the expanse of the English-speaking world; they would be circling the globe, traveling over one year, without having to bother with a foreign language.

The soloists would be Virginia Root, soprano, and Nicoline Zedeler, violinist. Nicoline had just won two medals at Chicago Musical College and had been about to study in Europe when she decided to audition for Sousa. All the way from Chicago to New York the pretty blonde sat in the ladies' lounge, practicing with frantic abandon and to the amused bewilderment of passengers and crew. She knew she had to outplay one hundred applicants.

A world tour ought to start, and end, at home; and so Sousa's regular Willow Grove season was plugged as the first part of the trip. To play four concerts daily, for several weeks, as the Willow Grove schedule demanded, and in surroundings familiar to most of them, was the best way of warming up.

Sousa in person went to the railroad station to meet his new violin soloist. "This is the first time I've been met by a King," Nicoline said pertly and handed him a batch of trunk checks. Sousa counted 14. "Farewell gifts," she blushed. "You may pick one, young lady," Sousa decreed, "but make sure it's large enough for you to catnap on occasionally."

They opened at Willow Grove on August 14. After this engagement came a brief vacation which Sousa used for a final hunting trip in Maryland. Next, a monster concert at the Metropolitan Opera House was to launch them through the Central and Eastern States, and Canada—12 hectic weeks averaging 14 appearances a week. Mr. Quinlan came to New York for last-minute arrangements; they were dining when Sousa suffered a violent spell of ague.

He had caught malaria in the Maryland swamps!

Stuffed with quinine, he held out through a few concerts. But in New Haven he had to be carried from the podium to the hospital. Spirits were low. The men wondered whether their world tour would take them as far as aboard ship.

For two weeks they traveled north, Herbert Clarke conducting, until a weak and jittery Sousa rejoined them in Montreal. They had never been so glad to see the boss!

The mists of early winter had already settled over the swamps and marshes when Sousa paid a sentimental call to Washington. Since his mother's death two years before, his visits had been very few. Usually he rode in style, by carriage, through his native city, but this time he walked. He stood at the fence of the two-story brick house in which he had grown up, with the Capitol's dome and the Congressional Library's green roof as a backdrop; he took a short walk to the First Church of Christ where he had worshiped as a boy, and to the public school he had attended and never finished. While on the other side of the Capitol the city was developing into a modern metropolis, the Pipetown section had hardly changed.

The aging Billy Wagner's gunshop, now huddling in the shadow of the new House of Representatives, was still the meeting place of equally aging cronies. A visit to the store, and a few hours of shooting clay birds at the Analostan Gun Club, was routine for home-town visits; but this time he did it all more solemnly, as if on a pilgrimage, as if trying to relive his youth, adolescence, and early manhood, before taking off.

The head count gave 68 when the expedition left on the SS *Baltic* on Christmas Eve. Sousa took Jane and both daughters along to show them the world. The Clarke brothers brought their wives, Virginia Root her mother. The musicians looked forward to their vacation at sea, with auction bridge and deck games, and only one concert for the Sailors, Widows and Orphans Fund. The ladies joined the games wearing ankle-length coats, gloves, and veiled hats. Christmas night, the band wandered from cabin to cabin, serenading, their spirits kept high by the generosity of a wine merchant on board. Again on New Year's Eve they paraded through the ship, and in their wake marched passengers, stewards, and crew.

On a seedy New Year's morning they steamed into Liverpool harbor. Sousa and his many ladies went to their hotel in a private automobile. The men were directed to report for rehearsal at Queen's Hall next morning.

The band was slightly out of joint after a week's loafing and overeating, and victims of seasickness were still weak. Yet they recovered sufficiently to gross 22,500 dollars in the first week and then to start touring, leaving the pea-

178

soup fog of London for the dazzling green of Ireland. In the British Isles alone, an area roughly one thirtieth of the United States, they covered 4360 miles in nine weeks, playing 111 concerts in 65 cities.

In Myrta Dydvil, Wales, they had a moment of intense shock. The stage on which they played had had to be extended, and toward the end of the concert a thunderous collapse of the brass side sent Sousa and ten musicians crashing down seven feet, in dust and debris. Virginia Root dashed out of the wings, screaming, and panicky concert-goers made for the exit. But Sousa reappeared, rubbed his bruised shoulder, readjusted his eyeglasses, and gave the downbeat, undismayed by the fact that sawdust was irritating the players' throats and that some of them were still down below, fighting timber. It turned out that the carpenter who had enlarged the platform was also the local undertaker, and the dignified Britisher never managed to live down the band's mock accusation that he had been trying to get a two-way business.

Another accident, less spectacular but even more dangerous, occurred at their concert in Plymouth. When her turn came, an ashen-faced Miss Root crept onto the platform, struggled through her number, and gave no encore. Later, before the violin solo, manager Clarke announced a change of program because of Miss Zedeler's sudden indisposition. With concert halls being unheated in England, portable gas stoves had been placed in the dressing room of the pampered American girls. When Clarke fetched Virginia for her solo, he had to break in the door and found her near fainting. Nicoline was already unconscious. The stove had leaked.

On March 4 they were in Plymouth again, whole and

healthy. A few hours later they would leave for Capetown, 5776 miles away. Through the freezing drizzle and the opaque fog of the still-wintry city trooped the bandsmen to purchase tropical outfits. Sedate Britishers, used to seeing people buy sun helmets in winter and arctic equipment in the hot season, were puzzled by those foreigners whose uniforms looked quite unusual in the streets.

On the dock the party stopped in front of a tablet marking the spot from where the Pilgrim Fathers had started out. The band had several members of old English stock who could but think with awe of their ancestors who had taken such hazards so that their offspring might reap what they themselves had sown.

The SS *Tainui* had only one third of the *Baltic's* displacement, but it was scantily booked. The band felt as if they were traveling on a private yacht—a rather luxurious craft, with electric fans in the staterooms. The last thing they saw were the Stars and Stripes flying on a U.S. man-of-war moored in Plymouth harbor.

The weather cleared as they steamed into the Atlantic, heading south. The men practiced in their cabins, Sousa held several rehearsals on deck. When after refueling at Santa Cruz, in the Canary Islands, they sailed out again past the ancient Spanish fort, the band gathered on the afterdeck and struck up the Spanish, English, and American national anthems, and then, as a crowning termination, *The Stars and Stripes*.

Temperatures kept rising at a prodigal rate. In little more than a week they experienced winter, spring, and summer. Ten days out of Plymouth they had a scorcher in the best Washington style.

This was the first message from the Equator, bellyband of the globe, which they were now rapidly approaching. The thermometer soared to new highs; the comfortable twilights of dawn and dusk vanished as the sun rose and set almost vertically, illuminating the world with a sudden flash at 6 A.M. and dropping it into deep darkness, practically without transition, 12 hours later.

Bandsman Edmund Wall, who had crossed the Equator before, performed the rites of baptism of greenhorns; in Neptune's costume, assisted by crew members made up as nereids, he gave novices a thorough drenching.

Several times a dim line in the distance indicated that they were following the coast of an immense stretch of land, but for several days the vague contour remained all they could perceive of the Dark Continent and its miracles of which they had read in adventure stories.

Finally, on March 23, shortly before midnight, they reached Capetown, their African terminal, a beacon of city lights not much different from Boston harbor.

In the morning hours of March 24 the Sousa forces went ashore in strength. Feeling somewhat insecure, as if the solid pavement were a decoy for wobbly planks, men and women tapped their way to an array of carriages drawn by white horses which took them to City Hall for an official welcome.

All Capetown seemed gathered to meet the March King and his host. The Capetowners were a friendly people, and theirs was a beautiful, hospitable, modern city which had sprung up from the African wilderness on a wide semicircular bay. Table Mountain was the backdrop, often covered in the morning by a sun-lined sheet of clouds.

The climate of Capetown in March was like that of southern California in September, and light summer clothes were well in order. Accommodations were nice and inexpensive, and so was the food; room and board cost no more than $1.50 a day. Everybody saved from his salary.

Business was good. Four concerts in City Hall were sold out. The capacity crowds hailed Wagner selections, popular music, and Sousa marches, as always and everywhere.

On March 26 they started out again, proceeding in a northeasterly direction. Suburbs flashed past the windows of their special train. Cosmopolitanism fell behind as they entered the immense strange continent where only several years before the Boers had struggled against the English to maintain their independence and control of the riches of a land which their Dutch ancestors had settled. The bandsmen had read in newspapers about the theater of war; but now that peace had been restored—a peace that had turned South Africa into a new jewel in the British crown—it looked rather different from what they had expected. The tracks climbed steadily, the scenery was an alpine vastness of fields—grandiose and yet serene. Soldiers' graves flitted past, blockhouses that had protected railroads and bridges, small native villages of low mud huts covered with straw.

The aborigines were tall men, six foot or more, descendants of one of several warrior aristocracies among the colorful variety of African tribes. The Kaffirs were no longer soldiers; and after the Boer settlers had come and displayed superior martial efficiency, Kaffirs were not too highly respected in their own homeland. Hordes of Kaffir children gathered at small stations, running up and down begging for pennies. Placid adults, clad in nothing but flashy scarves, looked on. The bandsmen distributed change. Peddlers sold fruit: delicious grapes at two cents a pound, pineapples for six cents a dozen.

On March 27 they arrived in Kimberley, 647 miles from Capetown, and had their first concert that night.

Kimberley was the "treasurehouse of the world," the site of the legendary diamond mines, where, from blue clay dug at great depth and spread over acres of ground, the fabulous stones were washed, looking quite unspectacular when they emerged rough and uncut. These stones were Kimberley's wealth and its people's undoings. Had it not been for foreigners' greed for diamonds, the Kaffirs would have freely roamed the vastness on which the city now stood.

When the bandsmen visited the mines, riding in diminutive trolley cars through a network of tracks 12 miles long, they saw Kaffirs working, operating machinery and sifting material.

Native workers had to enlist for three to six months, during which period they had to live in company barracks from where tunnels led into the mines. There were no vacations and after the labor term expired everybody was thoroughly checked. The daily output of Kimberley was estimated at 400,000 dollars, an amount hardly paralleled in any other industry at the time. An object no longer than a man's thumb was worth a fortune. And it was not only the loss involved in thievery that frightened the operators. Diamonds were not consumer goods that could be freely pumped into an expanding market. A comparatively small oversupply could upset the carefully established balance and cause a disastrous price rout. To the bandsmen's great disappointment, diamonds could not be purchased at the mines; only one member obtained permission through some personal contact, and he paid the stiff American retail price.

Sousa would hardly have thought that his musical education would yet be expanded in an African mine. As early as 1896 he had written a suite, *Three Quotations*, the last movement of which was entitled "In Darkest Africa." He had given it the touch of a wild continent as he pictured it in his imagination, with a flavoring of familiar American rhythm. Now, one Sunday morning in the De Beers' plant, he saw tribesmen perform their traditional dances within the compound, a pantomime of pagan rite, battle antics, and savage emotion, underlined by a few instruments including a primitive wooden ancestor of the xylophone.

Sousa and his party were having dinner at their Kimberley hotel when a waiter approached him and said that a Kaffir wanted to talk with him. Sousa replied that he didn't know any natives, but the man, so the waiter said, insisted he had known Sousa in America. When Sousa eventually decided to see the strange caller, he actually turned out to be an old acquaintance, Jim Nelson, a former helper on Dick Sutherland's farm.

Jim had left home, lured by adventure and the glib talk of a local friend, and got himself a job on a boat to Africa. But the long voyage bored him and he was tricked into playing craps with the natives in the crew; evidently craps was also played in Africa, and even better than in North Carolina. Jim, stone broke and stranded in Kimberley, implored Sousa to give him a job.

Actually, the band needed a man to help with the luggage. The natives were powerful and eager but extremely inefficient. Struggling with 28 instrument cases, particularly with the very big ones containing the Sousaphone, the brass drum, harp and tympani, they collided with each other, stepped on many toes, and wound up in chattering chaos. Jim from North Carolina turned out to be an asset for Sousa in South Africa.

March 29 saw the band in Johannesburg, the Gold City. Another type of treasure was buried there, scientifically dug and processed as a first step on its way to cool vaults in many national banks. Heaps of yellowish dirt, as high as 150 feet, gave the landscape its character.

From Johannesburg they visited Pietermaritzburg, Krugersdorp, named after "Uncle" Paul Kruger, the legendary patriot-president of the Boer's Republic; and Pretoria, his home town.

On April 11, after a beautiful journey over mountains, they reached the eastern coast of the Cape. Here the same eternal expanse of water was called the Indian Ocean. They played in the Town Hall of Durban, a sumptuous white marble affair distinguished for its supersized organ, the largest of its kind in the world, which had been brought in parts from England and assembled on the spot.

After the concert, they were desperately pressed for time to reach their overnight boat to East London. The only available transportation were two-wheeled rickshaws drawn by Zulu-Kaffirs, enormous men dressed only in horns and girdle, magnificent specimens; every one of them would have been a prize attraction in a wrestling arena. Sousa improvised a contest, offering a prize for the fastest rickshaw. The huge men, holding their painted bodies like racing ostriches, seemed to run almost as fast as the fabulous birds.

The overnight boat ride was uneventful, but when they reached East London there was no dock, and the sea was so rough that launches did not go near the steamer for fear of collision. Wicker baskets, lowered from the deck by means of a derrick, deposited the weary travelers on the tugs. A special cheer went up when the Sousa family swung in mid-air.

It was Good Friday and their concert featured sacred music.

King Williamstown; Grahamstown; Port Elizabeth, hub of the ostrich feather market. Neat towns with fine stores and impressive public buildings, receptive audiences, friendly applause. And on April 19 they were in Cape-town again, ready to embark for Tasmania. Their boat, however, was late and they gave three concerts instead of one. This was a boon for the treasury; daily expenses averaged 2500 dollars, and there would be no earnings during their three weeks on the Indian Ocean.

On April 21 they waited for the SS *Ionic* in vain. Next morning she was reported to have arrived, but had anchored way out in the bay flying the yellow flag.

Smallpox!

The band's situation seemed hopeless. Their first Australian concert was scheduled for May 15. There wouldn't be another boat to Tasmania for a month. Unless they boarded the disease-infested vessel, they would have to cancel the first part of the Australian tour, probably without finding enough work in South Africa to fill the gap.

Sousa, port authorities, health department, and skipper engaged in frantic negotiations. At last an agreement was reached: Since all smallpox suspects had been removed to an isolated island and the ship fumigated from funnel to engine room, the bandsmen could board it at their own risk.

From the moment they circumnavigated the Cape of Good Hope, the trip was a trial, if not an ordeal. They traveled through lashing gales and driving rains. The ship tossed and plunged in an angry sea, and the stench of the disinfectant was nauseating. The SS *Ionic* lifted her bow 70 feet into the air, then fell back between the waves, which swamped the deck. Simultaneously she rolled from one side to the other, moving, so to speak, in corkscrew motions, which, one day, reached an angle of 45 degrees.

The men slept strapped to their beds, or rather they lay there, not knowing their heads from their feet and feeling nothing but their furiously rebellious stomachs.

Sousa nevertheless called a rehearsal and appeared on time, spick-and-span. Disciplined players staggered in, but they could do no better than keep to their chairs. And after the first few notes had sounded, Sousa came to realize that one couldn't play a wind instrument when seasick!

The ship's doctor could not be consulted. The poor man who had not only had the smallpox scare but also performed an emergency appendectomy and battled vainly to save a dying baby, was in bed with a nervous breakdown, nursed by Dr. Lowe, Sousa's tympanist. Willie Lowe was the hero of the hour. There seemed to be no limit to the amount of rolling and rocking he could take in stride to aid fellow strugglers. Mrs. Root was thrown with her face against a radiator and her nose was badly cut. The tympanist dressed her injury, and he kept climbing pitching stairs to distribute medicines among all those who moaned for them. Later he was rewarded by an official citation worthy of a Marine, and by a special bonus from Sousa, which pleased civilian Lowe.

Spirits rose when the storm briefly subsided and the boys emerged from their berths to put on blackface and stage a minstrel show, prefaced by a regular "street parade" in long coats and high hats.

May 10 was the last day of their trial. On May 11 the boat limped into Hobart, Tasmania, a name that now spelled relief to the battered Americans who previously had known it only as a brand of apples. A delay of 24 hours caused them to miss their first scheduled concert. But that same evening, without a rehearsal, after weeks of idleness and physical discomfort, and still feeling as if their chairs were bucking horses, they played for an appreciative audience and did well enough.

They were not yet secure on their feet, and their eyes were not yet accustomed to the placid sight of solid land adorned by dry verdure and steady mountains, when they had to board yet another steamer to carry them to Melbourne, Australia.

It was a friendly vessel, however. The first 60 miles led down the Taman River into a glorious sunset, and the overnight crossing of Bass Strait was a peaceful affair. Yet the land voyage was not at all comfortable. Hardly in port, they rushed to the railroad station to catch the train for Sydney, 580 miles away. Provinces of Australia had different railroad gauges, and at the border between Victoria and New South Wales they had to leave their sleepers and change trains, sitting up for the rest of the night, unkempt, hungry, and thoroughly fed up with any known type of transportation.

Almost everybody who played an instrument in Sydney and vicinity escorted the Sousa forces in their spectacular ride to Town Hall. The visitors rode in huge carriages decorated with the Union Jack and the Stars and Stripes, drawn by teams of six horses with superbly uniformed coachmen holding the reins. An immense brass band led the parade through streets lined with festive crowds. At

Town Hall a 60-piece band played throughout the reception and *The Stars and Stripes Forever* climaxed the musical part of the festivities.

During the three weeks that followed, they gave 27 concerts in Town Hall, all sold out. They were entertained in clubs and on boat rides and by the Music Association of Australia, an affiliate of the AFM. They also played in neighboring towns such as West Maitland and Newcastle.

Australia—Down Under—was the land of bands. Every year and in every major city, Australian bands competed for cash prizes of up to 5000 dollars; to win one brought immense prestige. Judges came all the way from England and no money was spared to make the contests spectacular events. The visit of the American model organization was far more than pure entertainment for the Australians; in every town its reception was on a grand scale, with touches of admiration and sportsmanship. Everywhere the American visitors were met by the combined bands of the region and escorted in triumph through the main streets. It happened not only in Sydney and Melbourne, Ballarat and Adelaide; even Toowoomba, with a mere 10,000 population, turned out several bands.

It was a strange feeling for the bandsmen to be serenaded, instead of being the ones who played. In America The Governor had always been in the limelight, but here, in Australia, all the bandsmen shared his popularity. "Why did I ever leave home?" they had moaned on the uncomfortable night train. "Why do I have to go back?" they began to say when, in Melbourne, they were greeted by a band of 450, with the strains of *The Stars and Stripes.*

Where this melody was played the banner itself seemed to float, the flag of home.

June had come, in the Southern Hemisphere the equivalent of the northern December. The temperature got chilly, and even though the climate is not severe in this part of Australia, the deplorable absence of steam heat made it appear colder than it was. The furs Jane bought in London came in handy. In Melbourne they played in a large hall appropriately called the Glaciarum. Steam came out of the bells of the trombones and cornets; fingers grew numb. One player took to sitting on his right hand before a solo, to keep it warm.

In Ballarat, where they gave two concerts on June 23 in skating-rink temperature, the men played in their overcoats and some instruments were half a tone flat. During the matinee Sousa had to be replaced at the stand. He had kept aloof from the general lamentations about the wintry summer, but he had suffered nevertheless, and already at the beginning of the concert he wondered whether he could carry through.

He was quite ill on the overnight trip to Adelaide, where their schedule included 11 performances in seven days. Willie Lowe ordered him into bed, yet Sousa dragged himself to every concert, conducted the first number, and listened to the rest from a box.

Audiences raved. So did the press. Reviewers praised almost everything, including the variety of programs and the capability of every man. "If Bach is the musicians' musician, and Czerny the students' musician, Sousa is the people's musician"; this was written in the seaport city of Brisbane from where they returned to Melbourne, for a farewell matinee on Monday, July 23.

Now their whirlwind tour carried them to New Zealand. Bad weather had been forecast for the three-day passage, but the elements had no respect for the meteorologist and insisted on keeping the skies clear. Food was good. The officers were handsome. Jane and the girls enjoyed themselves, while Sousa was in his cabin, entering figures in a huge book. The tour was so expensive that every small item had to be accounted for; not only the 15 pounds for Jane's furs or five of spending money for Priscilla, but even two shillings Helen had once received, or a small tip on the boat to Lancaster. All those figures were circumstantially painted into the book with Sousa's delicate handwriting, and "closed into the account of Sousa's Unrivaled Band."

Invercargill, southernmost town of the world, was a lovely place, neat, good to live in; and the people of Invercargill were no less hospitable than their Australian neighbors. A local band waited at the pier, and the auditorium was already packed before the players had left the harbor district.

Nobody could have guessed that trouble was looming. After the parade, as the bandsmen started unpacking, they discovered that several trunks were missing—those containing the trombones, tuba, and tympani. A frantic Mark Lyons arranged for special transportation back to the port, while local bandsmen, who had lingered backstage, dashed home to get their own instruments for the hard-pressed Americans. And while Lyons searched freight yards and depots, it turned out that the New Zealand instruments were built in higher keys, and that the American mouthpieces did not fit. Sousa started the concert nevertheless; by improvising haunting pianissimi and giving his players

191

opportunity to rely on their wits, he struggled through the first part of their program until Mark Lyons arrived with the trunks which he had located in a depot, marked for customs' inspection. Dr. Lowe's tympani were missing, however; they had remained on the boat and were cruising the southern waters. The New Zealanders never heard the full impact of the Sousa percussions.

Matinees in New Zealand were poorly attended; so poorly, in fact, that several had to be canceled. The pioneer people of this scenic country were not accustomed to abandon work in the early afternoon for the sake of pleasure.

Earnings were disappointing; except for Auckland, New Zealand towns were signposts of an accumulating deficit. Only from the sight-seer's angle was the country an asset; the splendor of the glaciers, freezing waters, snow-covered pine woods, reminded the band of majestic spots in the Rockies. New Zealand was a new land indeed, not yet quite comfortable and not yet rising to international etiquette.

The boat that took the band to the North Island was filthy and rat traps in the cabins were appropriate. At the concert the Governor of New Zealand, who should have known better, remained seated during the rendition of *The Star-Spangled Banner*, and with him, stiffly, sat his staff. This more than outweighed the courtesy of his attendance.

Everything considered, however, the Australasian tour remained a success. Sousa collected piles of laurel wreaths, a handsome baton, and a Maori greenstone; he had been entertained by the Military and Naval Bandmasters of New South Wales, and in Melbourne's Government House, by the Governor-General of the Commonwealth.

He had brought a new march along, which he originally had meant to name *The Land of the Golden Fleece*. In fact, the saga of the Golden Fleece had a different location and origin, but the stunning size of Australia's herds of sheep, and the huge income derived from the wool industry, seemed to justify the title. Sir George Reed, High Commissioner of Australia, however, whom Sousa invited to select the final name for his opus, called it *The Federal March*.

Their farewell concert in Auckland, on August 31, was their farewell to Australasia. New Zealanders gave them a splendid and noisy send-off at the pier.

On September 1 they left for Victoria, Canada, from the budding southern spring through the perennial tropical summer, straight for the northern fall.

A first herald from home: the paymaster exchanged their pounds into the good old U.S. currency, in which one need not perform mental acrobatics to figure out how many pennies there were to the dollar. And the next greeting from America reached them at dinner, in the form of Budweiser beer, especially stocked for Sousa's Unrivaled Band.

The cool drink was a welcome refreshment when, on the fifth day they entered the harbor of Suva, in the Fiji Islands, through lines of coral reefs. The SS *Makura* took on a cargo of 600 tons of raw sugar from local plantations. The sugar growers had attractive villas and there was even a Carnegie Library; however, Suva was not much more than a sprawling village, with a white population of 1200. It would hardly have paid to give a concert, but there was entertainment galore for the men.

Everybody vied to treat the visitors to the specialties of

the region, which included kava, a soft drink that looked like coffee and tasted like absinthe. At night 48 natives came aboard, half-naked, their bushy hair bleached with herbs and plastered down with lime. For two hours they sang and danced in strangely weird rhythms, and then concluded their show by lining up for a neat four-part rendition of *God Save the King*. His Britannic Majesty's loyal subjects, however, were not yet devotees of a civilization that barred cannibalism. The bandsmen heard many stories about the cruelty of backwood natives and their despicable rites. And when, despite The Governor's warnings, several musicians visited the backwoods in a hired carriage, the islanders ran toward them in a manner that prompted the men to return in a hurry lest they wind up as a stew.

On September 5 they crossed the 180th parallel, the dateline, which meant that the next day would be another September 5. This was one of the many minor thrills for Pacific travelers, but one of the bandsmen turned the subject into a legal controversy. He had been the only uncongenial member of the group, and not a very industrious one; but he was a fighting unionist who viewed all oddities from the angle of the pay envelope.

Now the man requested double pay for the double September 5. Sousa patiently explained that, traveling east, they had lost almost one hour a day, and yet had been paid in full; so, since they had been overpaid on that part of the trip, it was only fitting that this be compensated for on the return voyage.

Yet the man continued to argue and stir up trouble, and Sousa transferred the debate to the calm atmosphere of the captain's quarters. The captain explained that similar questions frequently arose in matters of insurance and commercial contracts, and that litigation usually was referred to the courts of the locality where the agreements had been signed. Sousa, who did not enjoy arguments even though he did not shun a fight, declared himself ready to reopen the matter in New York. The man, however, did not want to wait. He became so unpleasant that Sousa eventually discharged him in San Francisco. Later he learned that the musican had taken his complaint to a California Local which, however, shared Sousa's point of view and reprimanded the musician for his ignorance.

The spat about the dateline was the only blemish in the otherwise idyllic travel north. For one week they sailed under tropical skies and over unruffled waters brilliant and varied beyond imagination, in a balmy, invigorating air that mirrored the lofty beauty of creation. It was all relaxation and enjoyment. The "Washy Hose Band" gave a concert on deck; they were Sousa bandsmen all right, playing under Peter Buys who had named his selected group after the Washy Hose Company, the volunteer fire company of Conshohocken, Pennsylvania, his home town.

On September 8 they recrossed the Equator. There would be no ceremonies for the old seadogs they all had become, but general enthusiasm called for some celebration, and a fancy dress ball was held instead.

On September 12 Honolulu, brilliant sentinel of a rising U. S. world power, was the outpost of home. Hawaii would not miss the opportunity of hearing Sousa, and Sousa would rather have by-passed any other archipelago than these treasure islands. The Bijou Theater, an ingenious affair—a big roof supported by columns, open at the sides for the finest breeze in the world, sea water perfumed by a profusion of flowers—was occupied by their largest audience since Sydney. They were acclaimed by listeners, lavishly entertained by Shriners and Elks, and their boat delayed its departure to allow them to play an evening concert. A 50-piece government band and native dancers and singers saw them off. The girls looked like dreams come true and sang like cherubs. When the SS *Makura* left the harbor, the band swung into a national air, *Aloha Oe (Farewell)*, a love song attributed to Queen Liliuokalani. *Aloha Oe*, the haunting tune, followed the bandsmen way out into the dark ocean, sung by a suave, velvety, native voice.

The men had sweet dreams that night. But on the following morning they were shaken abruptly into reality when Edwin Clarke distributed the instruction sheets for their transcontinental tour. The North American continent was straight ahead, over an expanse of water that kept shrinking under the busy revolutions of a propeller.

On September 14 they rehearsed and played a charity concert. On September 16 an improvised "Sousa-*Makura* Minstrel Company," reinforced by cheerful amateurs whose names had as yet only appeared on the passenger list, made a one-night stand. And then they approached America. It started, Columbuslike, with weeds and birds, and continued, 20th-century style, with powerful lighthouse beams. On September 19 the travelers were in Victoria, Canada.

A jam-packed house in Victoria; a trip south along the Pacific coast; and then, on September 22, a station name read: Blaine.

The time was 11:40 sharp.

The men scrambled out to the platform and sent up a rousing cheer to Blaine—U. S. A.

In Seattle a band was at the station, playing *Home Sweet Home*. It appeared to the men that not even in Australia had they had such a reception.

They had been viewing some of the wonders of the world; but there was indeed no place like home, and it was not at all humble. The Shasta Sunset Route held its own among all the glorious sites they had seen. And here, on home soil, it was still the world tour. The Greek Theater in Berkeley provided settings no less spectacular than those of exotic islands; oil boom towns were as indicative of natural wealth as the diamond and gold mines of Africa; California orange-grove centers could impress even visitors from Hawaii with all its pineapple plantations.

Los Angeles, where they arrived on October 16, for a one-week stop, was the terminal for some of the players who had contracts with various symphony orchestras for the full winter season. Sousa had approved of their leaving 8514 zigzag miles short of the ultimate goal, in order not to stand in the way of men who had found work for a longer period than he could offer.

The rest of the world tour actually was the twentieth transcontinental trip of Sousa's Band, and as such an impressive lesson on the country's industrial growth. Phoenix, Arizona, had become the site of a fantastically expanding rubber industry that helped Henry Ford put America on wheels. A few months could produce amazing changes. Even the cattle herds of Texas seemed to have multiplied since the men had last been there. And there were changes of climate at home as there had been at sea. In California, they experienced a heat wave with an equatorial touch and, two weeks later, in Wisconsin, a blizzard.

The routine of the transcontinental tour, however, did not much differ from that of its predecessors. In a way it was an anticlimax after the permanent excitement of the last year. But it was a placid anticlimax, with various friendly interludes. In Chicago, Simone Mantia, an ex-member who had joined the Pryor outfit, borrowed a Sousa uniform and joined the trombonists when they marched up front for their solo. In Grand Rapids, Michigan, 500 school children sang *The Stars and Stripes Forever*.

In Albany, New York, Sousa delivered a little speech to his men to express his thanks and appreciation. The Hippodrome, New York City, saw their last performance. The house was packed. Salvos of applause and a horseshoe of flowers six feet high greeted the leader. Then one week of recording for the Victor Talking Machine Company, and it was all over: 474 concerts; audiences totaling over one million; 47,213 miles on land and sea, between the 57th parallel north and the 47th south, with a business turnover of 600,000 dollars.

In some 50 home towns, U. S. A., Sousa bandsmen on furlough were local celebrities. In New York The Governor received friends and reporters and gathered headlines. It was another big feather in his cap.

And yet, home was best.

Proud but relieved, Sousa shouldered his gun and went back West, trap-shooting.

chapter twenty-one

O N SOUSA's order, a Boston jeweler made medals commemorating the tour. "Around the world with Sousa, 1910-11," was stamped on the upper and lower edges of the octagonal form; in the center were the two hemispheres, laurel branches, and two goddesses with musical instruments; on the reverse side was the name of the recipient and the assignment he had had on the tour.

Sousa distributed the medals, dedicated *The Federal March* to "our friends, the Australasians," and gave his blessings to the matrimony of Nicoline Zedeler and Emil Mix, the only marriage ever made within the band. In a new three-part symphonic suite *Tales of the Traveller* he described his impressions of Africa and Australia, and a fictitious promenade back home on the White House lot. This was like putting a dot on the *i*, or writing *finis* under a chapter. He never again went overseas.

It was not only the outbreak of war in Europe that kept him at home. He was nearing 60, and he was a grandfather, "Jack" Sousa having married immediately after graduating from Princeton in 1904. And as if to emphasize his decision to settle down, Sousa bought a house in Port Washington, Long Island, that he had rented several summers in the past. It was a stately mansion on Sands Point, with landscaped gardens sloping down to the Sound. Now, at last, he had all the wall space he needed for his photographs, oil portraits, citations, hunting trophies, and for his library of several thousand volumes all of which he could boast to have read. Now too the Sousas had a residential address; the nearest thing to permanency they had had in some 20 years had been two vaults in the Manhattan Storage Warehouse.

In a spacious, slightly old-fashioned room on the second floor, Sousa's heavy desk stood by a window overlooking the bay. Lifting his eyes from papers, books, and scores, he could see the gay white dots of sailing yachts in the distance; or he could watch his wife below, transforming the neglected garden into a profusion of flowers blazing with color. Although she employed a gardener, Jane did most of the planning and planting herself. Her own tastes and talents came to the fore, found a creative outlet, as she dug into the ground, put seeds and tender plants into waiting soil. Sousa's mind was at rest when he saw her busy and happy. Surrounded by beauty, by visual harmony, his desk was an ideal place for work, contemplation, decision. And it rapidly turned into a focal point of American musical policy.

For a good many years Sousa had been waging his private war against the phonograph, even though he had been among the first to make recordings. In an article entitled "The Menace of Mechanical Music," which appeared in *Appleton's* magazine in September, 1906, he predicted gravely that music teachers and instrument makers would be driven out of business, that amateurs would be discouraged, that the colorful country bands would vanish, and that even romance and matrimony would suffer, all this with detrimental effect on the happiness of the community. Sousa, at this point, failed to see the potentialities of the phonograph as a disseminator of good music. He only saw a "mathematical system of megaphones, wheels, cogs, disks, and cylinders," and more "revolving things," "wage an assault on personality." "Canned music," he said derisively, was as incongruous by a campfire as canned salmon by a trout brook.

Few of the many people to whom "canned music" is a household phrase realize that it was Sousa who coined it, brooding in a Boston hotel room while on tour, worried over the outcome of a congressional hearing on a new copyright bill at which he had testified. The issue of whether or not recording companies could help themselves to copyrighted music without paying royalties was coming to a head. A short time before, a composer had lost a suit on the grounds that a perforated paper roll did not represent a copy of his staff notation. And with the amazing development of the machine and its distribution, composers felt grievously victimized.

Sousa, of course, also considered this practical issue—the sale of sheet music on which he made money vs. the sale of records on which he didn't—when he took up his case against the phonograph. "Fair play to music and fair play to musicians," he said, were inseparably connected in the issue.

In Washington opponents argued that under the existing laws composers had no rights to mechanical reproduction. One gentleman went so far as to say that he would not have bothered to develop the reproducing apparatus had he anticipated that composers might cut in on his profits. When Sousa asked him whether his technical patents were not protected against unauthorized exploitation, he answered emphatically in the affirmative, yet failed to see why the same principle should apply to composers and their creative work. Sousa had been rather discouraged by the meeting.

But after the world tour, spurred by the fantastic distribution of his recordings which he had seen in Australia and Africa, he went to the Capitol to speak to a Senator, who, however, had never heard of Sousa, mispronounced his name, and promised nothing. This was rather an anticlimax after the personal triumphs in foreign lands.

The phonograph was not the only culprit, however. Night life on Broadway was developing at whirlwind pace. Night-club orchestras and singing waiters barefacedly exploited the hit tunes of the day. Years before, in England, on the request of a British music publisher who was counting on the impact of the visitor's name, Sousa had come out against musical piracy in two newspaper articles, only to find conditions at least as bad at home. The American copyright law actually antedated the Constitution, but its enforcement was nil.

The answer, eventually, was the founding of ASCAP, which grew into a world-wide organization collecting and turning over to composers payment for the use of their copyrighted music. The American Society for Composers, Authors, and Publishers was conceived one winter night in 1913, when Victor Herbert went to Shanley's Restaurant after a performance of *Sweethearts*, found the orchestra playing this same music, remembered he was getting nothing for it, and lost patience. His lawsuit dragged on for several years, with Shanley's contending that such music was not "for profit" and therefore, according to the law, not subject to royalties. When Judge Oliver Wendell Holmes finally ruled that "if this music weren't for profit it would not be there," ASCAP was already shedding its swaddling clothes.

Victor Herbert's friend John Philip Sousa was among the nine who met at the Lambs, and later at Luchow's, to discuss the charter. Throughout its early history, which was mainly one of dramatic litigations, the Society benefited by Sousa's active interest.

So Sousa had become a New Yorker, a suburbanite. He did not go on tour in the fall of 1915. While he had been conducting at the San Francisco Panama-Pacific Exposition, he had signed a contract with the New York Hippodrome, which would keep him in the city from September through May.

Sousa's Band was one of the prize acquisitions of Charles Dillingham, who had just taken over the Hippodrome from the Shuberts. The band was to participate in a show twice a day, Monday through Saturday, and provide the entire entertainment Sundays. Sousa turned the Sunday features into big events. His guest artists were leading opera stars like Emmy Destinn, Mme. Melba, Julia Culp, Maggie Teyte, Olive Fremstad, John McCormack; Ernest Schelling, then still touring as a pianist, played; once Sousa had Charlie Chaplin, rather new from England but already in the limelight, go through the motions of conducting a Suppé overture. On another occasion he had 15 different composers, among them Jerome Kern, Irving Berlin, Rudolf Friml, Oscar Hammerstein and himself, at 15 pianos, each playing, in turn, his own hottest hit, accompanied by the others; and Sousa cheerfully claimed the distinction of being the worst pianist of the lot.

The movies drained the business of vaudeville; the tango superseded the two-step; the age of jazz loomed. Yet the popular fancy for marches seemed unaffected by fashion. "Marches will be the music of the world as long as men like to keep in step," Sousa proclaimed from his suite at the Hippodrome Building where he rested between shows.

Sousa's birthday this year was turned into a virtual holiday when Dillingham arranged for orchestras and bands in practically all parts of the country to play, simultaneously, Sousa's newest march. On November 6, 1915, at 3:45 P.M. sharp, New York time, the *New York Hippodrome March* was struck up in Chicago and Texas, in Boston, Philadelphia, and San Francisco, in Cleveland and St. Louis, by the Marine Band in Washington, and by army bands the country over, while Sousa was on the Hippodrome podium receiving a cigar humidor made of 1274 dimes, contributed by the 1274 Hippodrome employees, from scrubwoman to executive. The committee, which included Walter Damrosch and Leonard Liebling, representing American musicians and music critics respectively, was headed by William Courtleigh, Shepherd of the Lambs, who made the presentation and said that Sousa "had placed the entire country under a lasting obligation and has merited deepest debt of gratitude for having for so many years thrilled the heads, hearts, and even the heels, of all the people."

Reporters always crowded the Hippodrome and occasionally ventured out to Sands Point. Sousa was a gold mine for a news-starved interviewer; and, if caught in the right mood, he could talk about a prodigal number of issues. You could always rely on the March King if you were short of lines. Sousa did not mind the question-and-answer game for the benefit of the newspaper reader, and sometimes he enjoyed himself hugely when reading what he had said off the cuff.

Once he said, in perfect seriousness, that he was discussing all his affairs with his old horse Marguerita, which never gossiped, never talked back. At other times he might develop his philosophy of the "root man," who would supersede the current species of humans who had exhausted their capacities of achievement; the newcomers would not be "an evolution from man as we know him, but a new type arbitrarily created to serve the purpose of God, Providence, and Nature, or whatever it might finally be decided to call the infinite." Thus read an item in the New York *Press*.

Sousa liked the latest ladies' fashions, he volunteered; the short skirts which, at long last, revealed the shapeliness of American female legs; and he expressed hope that they would never again fall so low as to obscure the novel attraction.

Or he might talk about cooking. Spaghetti with meat balls was his favorite dish. The nation learned that Mr. Sousa wanted his tomatoes to boil for a solid three hours, the meat balls to be added precisely at the halfway mark, three bay leaves precisely 30 minutes later; that the spaghetti (not macaroni, please!), must be slid into the water very carefully lest they break, and must boil precisely 20 minutes, no more, no less, so they be tender—neither tough nor doughy. And Mr. Sousa wanted hand-grated Parmesan cheese on the side; not the bottled type.

The only question he seemed at a loss to answer was which of his marches he liked best. "All of them," he might say vaguely, "or, rather, the last one written." Actually, it had become an established fact in the Sousa family that Father never emerged from his study after finishing a new composition without the solemn proclamation that this was the best thing he had ever done.

If the outbreak of war in Europe did not immediately affect Sousa's life, it occupied his thoughts a great deal. He knew the world better than most other Americans, and had been equally happy in both parts of the camps divided.

"The tragic thing about this war is that it is a family war," Jane would say, recalling the late King Edward's German ancestry and slight accent.

Sousa well remembered the murdered Archduke Francis Ferdinand from the Chicago World's Fair, where the heir to the Austrian and Hungarian thrones had come on a good-will mission to promote commerce. He remembered him as a tall and handsome bachelor in his thirties, whose stiffness had disappointed Fair visitors just as it had disappointed the ladies of Montana, Utah, Colorado, and Nebraska. Even the officials at the Austrian pavilion had had to admit that their future monarch should have been better briefed before coming to America, where the display of elusive hurry did not fit into the notions of a waltz-happy smiling capital on the banks of the Blue Danube. And now the Prince and his wife were dead, and the bullets of the assassin had touched off the greatest war in history.

Sousa's sweeping internationalism, as expressed after his first tour abroad, had not always been followed consistently in word and deed. In 1910, in his third excursion into the best-selling pastures of book writing, he had stated:

"I don't believe in an alliance between America and any other country. We are strong and powerful, and prosperous enough on our own account . . . It is doubtful to me if an alliance with any other nation, amounting in effect to a trust of nations, would be any more advisable than the business trusts which are becoming so common . . ." The opus, *Through the Year with Sousa*, was an anthology of sorts, actually a calendar in which appears, under each date, the birthday of some great musician and a Sousa quotation, or a few bars of Sousa music, or some line from a Sousa song or verse. Apparently made at random, the selection is significant because made by Sousa himself.

Part of Sousa's philosophy was that musical creation knew no boundaries, that there was no such thing as national music; yet he would insist that American composers were by no means influenced by music from abroad. Or, his three foreign decorations pinned over his heart, he would proclaim that he would never hire a foreign soloist. "No imported musical talent for me," he was quoted as having said. "American artists are good enough."

And yet, even in apparent contradiction, Sousa was completely sincere. He loved all the world, but he loved America best.

Early in 1916, when indications were that the United States might enter the conflict, Sousa offered his services to organize military bands. The offer was duly appreciated and kept on record.

Meantime entertainment continued as usual. In mid-October, 1916, Sousa's and Pryor's bands faced one another in a most unusual benefit performance: a baseball match on the Long Branch, New Jersey, diamond. On November 6 Mr. Dillingham organized a music festival at the Philadelphia Opera House, Sousa's Band appearing in celebration of another Sousa birthday. Another pool of dimes had been made into a loving cup; the centerpiece of the banquet table was a miniature stage with 50 figures representing Sousa's Band in operation.

On the occasion Sousa himself gave a present this time: a march dedicated to the Boy Scouts, a large detachment of whom came to Philadelphia for the presentation. In his address Sousa told the youngsters that his marches had drawn their basic inspiration from war—the Civil War, when he had been tramping behind the blue-clad recruits. Unlike most boy-dreams, he added, his dreams to lead a military band had come true.

And then, on April 6, 1917, the United States was at war.

Late in May, in Chicago, Sousa was sworn in as a Navy lieutenant, attached to the Great Lakes Naval and Recruiting Station, in charge of military music.

Lieutenant Sousa was granted a furlough until such time as he would have honored his current contracts.

These contracts included a concert in Toronto. The program featured the national anthems of all the Allied countries. *The Star-Spangled Banner* stirred up applause stormy even by the standards of those days in which excitement ran high. Glancing around, Sousa saw two young Canadian soldiers in the front row, both on crutches, leaning against each other for support. They both had lost one arm—one the left, the other the right—and their remaining two hands joined in vigorous clapping. It was a weird sight, and yet the infirm soldiers apparently enjoyed themselves; they laughed heartily, happy at their ingenuity that had overcome, for the first time perhaps, a handicap that might have dropped others into an abyss of despair.

On September 9 Sousa gave his last concert in Willowgrove, ending his professional career for the duration. On September 10 the band disbanded until further notice. They would have celebrated their Silver Anniversary on September 25; but while the occasion was marked by articles in the musical press, The Governor was in Kansas City, conducting recruit bandsmen during Old Glory Week in Electric Park and premièring, in semimartial settings, his *Naval Reserve March*. In the audience sat a nostalgic former President Theodore Roosevelt who now watched the holocaust from the sidelines and gave praise to Sousa's music and to his uniform.

Colonel Roosevelt too knew a great deal of the world, and also about the enemy, Kaiser Wilhelm, whom he had met abroad, when they were both on horseback and the old Rough Rider had been more than an equal to the boisterous monarch who used a replica of a saddle for a desk chair, claiming that this inspired him.

On his induction papers, Sousa had given his profession as "composer, novelist, conductor of Sousa's Band." But soon Lieutenant Sousa displayed organizational skills which might have caused the envy of field-ranking professionals. The Great Lakes Naval Station had had a band of 75 when he was sworn in; several weeks later they had some 600 enlistments.

Sousa knew how to cope with the perplexing problem of handling great numbers of men. He would not form new cadres, as general staff men might have done, but organized a battalion of about 350 musicians, with himself as commander, and divided it into "double battleship units" instead of companies. Out of this pool he could form ensembles of practically any size, supply reserve men for any instrument, and reorganize bands numerous enough for regimental purposes. Whenever the Navy Department needed a band, Lieutenant Sousa could provide it on short notice. Admiral Henry T. Mayo, Commander of the Atlantic Squadron, expressed admiring astonishment about a band that could start a concert one hour after reporting for duty; such an achievement, he commented, was unprecedented in all the services he had known.

It was a thrilling experience to work with young people again. Few of Sousa's men were over 25; they were no exceptional musicians but had had some experience with college or community bands and possessed boundless enthusiasm. For them, Sousa selected the easiest and most effective of his parade marches, old hits like *The Thunderer*, *Semper Fidelis*, *High School Cadets*, *The Washington Post*. His was indeed the largest and handsomest marching band of the war. Lieutenant Sousa donned his white navy cap, exactly as regulations required, lifted his saber to his shoulder, and glanced fondly at the two stripes on his cuff. "Lieutenant" wouldn't have been very much 30 years ago, when he had coveted a commission; for a sexagenarian it was at least unusual.

Actually, his functions were those of a major, and not confined to routine.

Secretary of the Treasury William Gibbs McAdoo wanted a marching song characteristic of this war, expressing American determination "to make the world safe for humanity." Sousa promised to try. It would not only have to be a military strain; the humanitarian angle would have to be emphasized, and the composition should be effective in the sense of the Treasury which had to raise astronomic amounts to keep the war going.

Inspiration came at dinner in Kansas City. It came so suddenly and overwhelmingly that Sousa hurriedly jotted the melody on his cuff. He worked on the march all night, and yet another night, and on the train back to Chicago. And in October, when the First Liberty Loan Parade marched through New York's Fifth Avenue, the *Liberty Loan March* made its rousing debut.

The country needed more ships. Ships had to be built faster, much faster than U-boats could sink them. They would have to carry the strongest expeditionary force in history to shores some 3000 miles away and keep it supplied with staggering amounts of matériel; 250,000 men were needed to form a "shipbuilding reserve" and Sousa marches were unmatched recruiters. "I shall do anything in the world to put more ships on the seas flying the Star-Spangled Banner," Sousa had buoyantly promised, and he was as good as his word.

In November, at the Hippodrome, he led the combined bands of the Atlantic Fleet in *The Volunteers*, the new march dedicated to the shipbuilders of America and their new wartime head, Edward N. Hurley. It was an unusual composition for a wartime march; Sousa had purposefully hunted for a lilting melody, for an attractive, joyous, optimistic tune to fit the situation, for something to embody the idea of barbaric splendor. He was a peaceful man at heart, but once the country was at war one had to join in wholeheartedly.

"I have had many triumphs in my life," he would say, "but my greatest ambition is to lead a band down the

Kaiser Wilhelmstrasse in Berlin, playing *The Star-Spangled Banner*." Little did he know that the German recruits, who soon would come to grips with American trainees, were drilled to the tunes of his own marches. Sousa's old hits had become so thoroughly integrated into German bands that the younger generation did not realize they were of enemy origin.

On November 23 Lieutenant and Mrs. Sousa went to the opera. There was nothing unusual in Philip leaving during intermission; even his rather belated return after the lights had been dimmed did not seem extraordinary to Jane—her husband knew so many people. But after the curtain had fallen, the singers had taken their bows, and the lights had gone on, she uttered a cry: the naval officer who helped her into her coat was nearly clean-shaven; he had no beard, no whiskers, merely a thin mustache . . . "I paid a visit to the barber in the building," Sousa explained. "This is a young men's war!"

Working with young men was a fountain of youth. A few days after the procedure at the opera house which made newspaper headlines and family history, a chubby-chinned Sousa took 200 of his boys to a clambake at Coney Island. The breeze was stiff, the surf rough, the sand battered by gusts and waves. The boys had gathered most of their nautical experience on the Mississippi or on the lakes of Wisconsin and Minnesota; those navy recruits actually had never breathed air permeated with salt water, had never heard the gushing sound of waves, had never seen a clam in a shell. One cornetist had seriously asked whether oysters grew on bushes or in gardens, like most other stuff that came in cans. But Sousa, the rejuvenated old seadog, could tell the landlubbers all about the ocean and the elements and the stunning phenomena they produced between Coney Island and Tasmania. He liked to relive those distant travels.

Wherever a patriotic drive was held—Liberty Loan drives, Red Cross drives—Sousa and his battalion marched in the vanguard. From all over the country millions poured into various funds. Individuals might pledge up to 200,000 dollars to hear Sousa conduct some patriotic air. His baton might be auctioned off for as much as 400 dollars. Mendelssohn's *Elijah*, performed under Sousa's baton by a huge band, famous singers, and a chorus of 10,000, on the New York Polo Grounds, was a highlight of his conducting career, a venture he might never have undertaken except for the War Thrift Festival.

The war netted the March King yet another title: they called him "Pied Piper of Patriotism."

Once, in Detroit, Sousa and his recruits seriously interfered with legal procedure. They were scheduled to march past the court building, and an understanding judge had allowed a five-minute recess to permit jurors to watch the parade from the window. But one juror, a withered old man with a flowing white beard and distant Civil War reminiscences, was irresistibly drawn out of the courtroom and into the street. Bent, and hobbling on his cane, he trailed the band on its way downtown, and a deputy sheriff had to take up pursuit to bring the band-struck oldster back to jury duty.

Also in Detroit Sousa marched his men to a hotel to serenade one of the most important figures of war production, Charles M. Schwab, the steel magnate. Mr. Schwab acknowledged that Sousa's naval band was better even than his own Bethlehem Steel Work Band, which he had thus far considered to be the best in the world.

Sousa's creative output, much reduced in number during the years of constant traveling, was again stimulated by war and the promise of peace. As virile and swinging as ever, his marches poured forth, suggesting advance, strength, self-confidence: *Anchor and Star, The Chantyman's, Flag of Freedom, Sabre and Spur, Solid Men to the Front, U. S. Field Artillery.* He wrote a great choral work, *The Last Crusade,* inspired by a poem by Alice Higginson about the Allied conquest of Jerusalem in 1917. He wrote the music to a poem of his own, *Great Lakes;* to another by Lieutenant Colonel John McCrae, *In Flanders Fields the Poppies Blow;* to a third, by his daughter Helen, who had become Mrs. Hamilton Abert, *When the Boys Come Sailing Home.* He wrote a new band arrangement of *The Star-Spangled Banner* and an *American Wedding March,* dedicated to the American people and composed on the request of the American Defense Scouts Committee, to discourage the use of Wagner's or Mendelssohn's.

Sousa and his men went unscathed through the first assault of the greatest killer of World War I—the Spanish influenza. Thanks to the efficiency of a young battalion physician, they could continue traveling, drumming up money for the Treasury. Early in November they were detailed to Toronto to boost the Canadian Victory Loan campaign. They crossed the border less than 24 hours before the armistice was signed.

The flu caught up with Sousa in Toronto. It was a comparatively mild attack, but he ran a high fever and an abscess in his ear caused him constant pain. The news that the Germans had signed the armistice on Allied terms, in

Marshal Foch's sleeping car in Compiègne, enthused him. Until the very last moment many people had thought that the campaign would continue well into 1919, causing further grievous losses.

In January, 1919, Sousa obtained his discharge. The Victory Medal and the Order of Veterans of Foreign Wars followed in due course.

In February, 1920, Sousa was a guest of honor at the Pennsylvania Military College, which had conferred upon him an honorary doctorate of music. Another honorary graduate of the day was Senator Warren G. Harding, who sat near him at dinner and turned out to have played the tuba in his home community of Blooming Grove, Ohio, before starting on the long road that was to lead him into the White House.

Returning from Pennsylvania, Sousa found a letter from the Navy Department. Thomas Washington, Rear Admiral, U.S.N., notified him of his promotion to lieutenant commander.

This was not bad, after all, even for a young "Doctor" of 65!

Friends now took to addressing him as commander, and he relished it.

chapter twenty-two

ANY felt that Sousa's audiences had never been so large, his programs never so varied and modern, as when he took to the road again with his reassembled band after the war.

The Roaring Twenties were on. Flippancy, exaggeration, artificiality, were in fashion. Clad in long black stockings and tasseled narrow skirts, well-bred young ladies performed the craziest dances, twisting their bodies to twisted rhythms. In the whirl of postwar affluence and postwar hysteria, Sousa stood like a pillar of clean-cut, sturdy, healthy Americanism. His concerts brought a fresh breeze into an atmosphere supercharged with new notions like neurosis, speak-easy, flapper, and jazz. The March King was refreshingly old-fashioned.

One day in 1920 he stepped into Centemeri's Fifth Avenue shop and ordered 7200 dollars' worth of white kid gloves, custom-made, 100 dozen, at six dollars a pair. A flabbergasted clerk said that this was the largest order on record in the retail business ever. The story spread like wildfire. Commander Sousa, it became known, was about to start on the longest continental tour of his career and did not want to run short of gloves. People declared that superstition kept him from wearing the same pair twice. Actually, Jane had once had one pair cleaned, and it had been returned too tough, without the elasticity that Sousa's hands needed. He wore his gloves tight and had to have them as pliable as skin for his method of conducting, in which the flecking of a muscle might be significant.

Sousa was also an extraordinary customer for shoe-makers. He had his footwear custom-made at the then-fabulous price of up to 125 dollars a pair; and he owned nearly 100 pairs, from slippers to hunting boots. He liked shoes, he might explain. Sousa was proud of his small feet.

After the Sousas established residence, the community of Port Washington never ran short of gossip. The commander received visitors sitting cross-legged on the sofa; he had found this to be the most relaxing position. He wrote letters just in one panel down the right-hand side of the paper, his delicate handwriting filling the narrow margin; nobody really knew why. And he might put the address into verse, puzzling busy postal clerks on both sides of the Atlantic; he liked to write verse.

And there was still another story that had kept people guessing and gossiping for a long time: his very name. Rumors had it that he was an immigrant from Greece or perhaps Germany; and that "Sousa" was the combination of the letters S.O. with the destination U.S.A., marked on his luggage. He had been John Philip So, or John Filipso, some said; from Germany emanated a version that he was one Sigismund Ochs, from the Rhineland; British sources ventured that he had been Sam Ogden, a famed Yorkshire musician. In ancient Greece seven cities had once vied for the distinction of being recognized as the birthplace of Homer; fans of at least three foreign nations now tried to make Sousa their compatriot.

This puzzling story was, in fact, a brainchild of Colonel

Hinton who had run out of Sousa anecdotes in the thick of a tour. It turned out to be one of the most effective publicity stunts ever devised. It made the rounds not only in daily and musical papers, but also in farm, labor, trade, even religious, periodicals. Sousa was asked about his name in practically every town, country, continent; he was provoked into emphasizing his Americanism at every interview and dinner party. Now, after three decades of it, he still wearily denied the story, mildly apologizing for having to kill a good anecdote.

Around the house, Sousa was relaxed and extremely informal, nothing like the trim militaristic figure the public saw. He wore casual clothes and liked none better than his battered hunting outfit. Sometimes, before driving into town, his wife or daughter had to remind him that he should not put in an appearance in mismatched clothes. Visitors had the impression that he always spoke in light jokes, good-naturedly teasing everybody all the time.

He did not want anybody to challenge his own seriousness, however. Olin Downes, then a young music critic with the Boston *Post*, stayed at Sands Point for several days to gather material for a series of articles on Sousa. Once at breakfast he answered one of his host's statements with a polite, "Yes, Mr. Sousa, that is correct." Sousa sat back stiffly: "Young man," he lectured, "I am not in the habit of making incorrect statements!"

In 1922, at Willow Grove, Sousa was thrown from his horse and hurt his back. After that he was almost constantly in pain. "It's pretty tough," he admitted to friends who mentioned his affliction. It was agony to raise his arms; so he took to conducting below the waist. But he was very angry when someone suggested that he take it easy, if not

retire. "The first you'll hear of Sousa's retirement is w
you read 'Sousa dead!' " he might retort. "A man kee
going by keeping going. When he retires . . . he dries u
like a plucked flower and blows away." And he insisted
that he would continue touring until he had traveled one
million miles with his band.

And this is how his younger fans were to remember him:
a stocky, militaristic figure, a fringe of white hair below a
bandmaster's cap, square-shouldered, impeccably straight,
moving his hands with grace and restraint, giving cues often
by the mere raising of a thumb. "If people like acrobatics
let them see vaudeville," he said, in obvious contrast to his
earlier statements about having to act out one's music,
rationalizing, but never admitting, his slight handicap.

In May, 1923, John Philip Sousa met Thomas A.
Edison.

Dr. James Francis Cooke, of Philadelphia, who headed
the John Church Company which published Sousa's most
important compositions, told him that America's most famous inventor had wished to make the acquaintance of
America's most famous composer. And so one day Dr.
Cooke and Sousa drove to the Edison Laboratories, in
West Orange, New Jersey.

Edison was seven years older than Sousa. He had invented the phonograph in 1876, when Sousa was still fid-
dling in theaters, and he had demonstrated the electric
lamp on New Year's Eve 1879, one year to the day before
Philip and Jane got married. Their eyes twinkled and their
motions were sprightly as they shook hands, as if they were
old friends who had not seen each other for a while and
had many things to talk about.

Edison was almost deaf. Sousa, on and off troubled by

his ear, was temporarily hard of hearing. Dr. Cooke acted as interpreter to spare them the exertion of shouting. First Sousa managed to make a few flattering remarks about the phonograph, which, after all, had carried his fame around the world. But soon Dr. Cooke found himself shouting a heated argument back and forth.

"Each man spoke his own thoughts and with vehement frankness," he later wrote in *Etude* magazine of which he was editor. "Mr. Edison announced that in his opinion the music of Mozart was of little consequence. At this, Mr. Sousa bristled like a bulldog facing an enemy and made some remarks about the shortcomings of 'canned music.' [My] impression was that Mr. Edison thought that Commander Sousa would do well not to discuss electrical inventions and that Commander Sousa thought Mr. Edison had better reserve his opinions about music. They parted in excellent humor. It was a memorable meeting."

The Philadelphia Music Week of 1924 featured as its final event Sousa conducting his *The Last Crusade* at Wanamaker's Grand Court for 8000 people. After the performance the Philadelphia Orchestra's conductor, Leopold Stokowski, told the audience of his first arrival in the United States, when forlorn in summery New York he ventured into the Hippodrome where Sousa was giving a concert, and experienced one of the great impressions of his life.

"The music swept me off my feet," Stokowski said. "The rhythm of Sousa stirred me, for it is unique. I tried to analyze my sensations . . . The music had such wonderful regularity. Someone else might have such regularity, but he would not have the enormous drive and push. . . . From

that time on I always wanted to meet him, that musician with a pirate's beard. . . .

"They say that genius is doing something better than any other person does it. Sousa is such a genius. He is a genius whose music stands supreme as a symbol of the red-bloodedness of humanity."

Yet, gradually Sousa's schedule had to ease and to follow a more regular pattern. He auditioned and rehearsed in June and toured from July until Christmas; in January he went South for sports, and traveled North in the wake of spring, for several weeks of composition, gardening, and rest in Long Island.

"Rest" included such chores as the writing of his third short novel, *The Transit of Venus*, with the background of a scientific expedition undertaken in 1882; and of his autobiography, an informal and amusing mixture of thought, reminiscence, and incident, which appeared in 1925 in *The Saturday Evening Post* and later, in 1927, in book form as *Marching Along*.

"Rest" meant the planning of the first American grand opera which he was yet determined to write, even though his latest stage work *The American Maid* (a revision of his earlier *The Glass Blowers*) written to a topical libretto by Leonard Liebling, had been a near-flop.

"Rest" also meant the writing of newspaper articles; the delivery of speeches; his presence at committee meetings and symposiums; and countless other activities in his clubs —the Republican Club, the Athletic Club, the Lambs, Elks, Shriners, and the Trapshooters Club, of which he was president for a number of years.

Sousa had always been in demand as an afterdinner speaker and he invariably did well, in contrast to the edgy, if not awkward, style in some of his writings. To express himself, whether in words or music, he needed listening faces, the personal contact with a live audience.

For this same reason he shied away from radio for a long time, much as he realized the influence of the new medium on cultural advance. "It fulfills its purpose, but its scope is limited," he wrote in *Marching Along*. "The rapport between performer and audience is invaluable and can be fully attained only through actual vision . . . I am reluctant to lose the warm personal touch with my audience."

Even though his seasons were growing shorter, Sousa still obtained the best musicians the country could supply. Most of the men held positions with symphony or radio orchestras, but when the Sousa tour opened they flocked back into the fold. To play for "the old man," as they now called him, was still the most coveted assignment; among the younger generation of musicians, to have been a Sousa bandsman was Open Sesame to top rank in the profession.

Sousa himself still liked nothing better than his own concerts. "My enthusiasm has never waned," he explained at the age of 71. "I get the same pleasure now when I step before my band as I did when I was just starting."

And yet he did not feel old enough to play golf.

In December, 1926, he spent again one week on horseback, riding from Hot Springs, Virginia, to Washington, the fifth time he had taken the 300-mile trip in this manner. His back ached and weather was foul throughout, yet he insisted that the outing had put him into first-class shape and that while fighting wind and sleet he had had an inspiration for a horseman's march. But he had no time to write it; he was too busy with his opera.

In the preceding summer he had written his most ambitious march to commemorate the one hundred and fiftieth anniversary of his country's birth. The *Sesquicentennial March* was not only a rousing functional composition; it was a tone picture in five parts, a series of dramatic scenes describing the writing of the Declaration of Independence. The customary five sections of the march described, in turn, John Hancock's solemnity and Richard Henry Lee's Southern soft-spokenness; the debate and acceptance of the Declaration; they gave a musical characterization of each member stepping forth to sign, before winding up with an energetic finale, symbolizing the young country's determination to be, and stay, free.

Traveling through the country, more at leisure now but acutely aware of developments, Sousa realized that he would leave a rich legacy. Bands mushroomed all over—in the smallest communities, the simplest schools. He was amazed to see that some were one third female and featured not only the customary concert instruments for solo performances but also tubas and trombones. While jazz almost monopolized paid entertainment, invaded dance floors and even concert halls, bands remained the stronghold of popular self-expression, of popular love of music, the poor man's philharmonic orchestra.

And, in addition, Sousa felt that the community band was invaluable in teaching discipline.

For many years he had predicted a great future for music in America—because of its commercial value. And to the comfort of those who might have taken exception to such materialism, he had specified that the country was "too young to go after art for art's sake," but that it would go after music if it paid; and honest music making did pay, as he had well experienced. His prophecy of nearly a generation earlier was coming true.

He was increasingly preoccupied with music for youngsters. He gave considerable time to Interlochen Camp, and would travel long distances to attend the debut of some children's band, or to conduct at schools or juvenile clubs, or to sit in a jury in band contests. As a juror he wasn't very helpful, however. He could not bring himself to disappoint youngsters, so he put down 100 for every contestant. The chairman ultimately tore up Commander Sousa's slips; to have had his name on the jury had been a privilege in itself.

Sousa had always had a soft spot for children. Many a Sousa-struck youngster of the eighties and nineties had become Sousa's friend, if not business associate. Taylor Branson, the lad who had hung about the bandstand at the dedication of *The Washington Post* was Marine Band leader. Frederick Gaisberg, who as a boy had occasionally held the March King's music on the stand on windy days, was an RCA Victor executive. The friendship with Dr. Cooke dated back to a concert at Manhattan Beach, when teenage James Francis had hiked from his Brooklyn home to hear Sousa perform two marches he had submitted, and Sousa, who had not known how young the composer was, had taken him to a swank hotel veranda for ice cream at the then-unheard-of price of 30 cents a plate.

One young bandleader had come up in New York, Edwin Franko Goldman, Nahan Franko's nephew, who had once brought Sousa a message from his uncle and had been in touch with him ever since. Goldman had started out as a cornet player with the Metropolitan Opera orchestra; in 1911 he had organized a military band; after the war he had started free band concerts on the campus of Columbia University, later moving to the Mall in Central Park. Sousa liked him.

One day, when Sousa visited Goldman, his host asked him whether he would care to see the little girl who had played for him in Washington some time ago. Sousa politely said yes. The door opened and tripping along came Goldman's septagenarian mother, nee Selma Franko, who had been concertizing with her brothers and sisters in that memorable year, 1869. "I remember you very well," Sousa exclaimed. "You wore a dark brown velvet dress and double braids!"

It was good to know that a member of a family with so fine and old a musical tradition would keep the banner of noble band music flying in a jazz-crazy world.

"The world is jazz-crazy," Sousa said in 1927. "My marches were written to two-step time, but the average American wants ceaseless change, and radio and victrola are working havoc with the sale of sheet music."

However, by then his *Stars and Stripes* had sold ten million copies in sheet music and 20 million recordings, and the Collector of Internal Revenue had claimed from him the then-fantastic amount of 12,000 dollars in 1926.

Jazz was the aging Sousa's pet grievance. He thundered against it, shrugged it off, laughed it off, called it names, and yet was helpless against the flashy upstart.

Sousa's feelings were shared by most older musicians of consequence. They had attended in strength the now-historic première by Paul Whiteman of Gershwin's *Rhapsody in Blue* in Aeolian Hall on Lincoln's Birthday 1924. It was the first time that jazz invaded the concert hall—a sacrilege that turned into a sensation. No one disputed

Gershwin's genius; but most agreed that there were too few composers of talent among those who turned out jazz. Sousa admitted that he had heard some who were great, even inspired; yet, there were many jazz writers he would not call composers. Too much of it was manufactured and mechanical to suit his taste.

He was appalled at advertisements offering to teach the noble art of jazz writing in 20 lessons. It hurt him to hear practically every good melody cruelly jazzed up. He had spent a lifetime making arrangements with loving care, anxious not to distort the character of a composition, avoiding music which did not lend itself naturally to adaptation for band. But disrespect seemed to have turned into a virtue in this disillusioned postwar world.

Inevitably famous composers were asked what they thought of jazz. In Italy the sexagenarian Pietro Mascagni exploded that the government ought to prohibit it. Mussolini was already in power, and Italians were becoming used to having the government mingle in the oddest things.

"That's all bosh!" Sousa exclaimed when he heard of it. "It would be just as sensible for the government to prohibit Mascagni!"

"What do *you* think of jazz, Commander?"

"Some of it makes you want to bite your grandmother," Sousa wisecracked. "But jazz—good, bad, indifferent—will live in popularity so long as dancers want it. It's hard on real estate owners. It allows 1000 dancers on a very constricted floor space. Modern dances remind me of a pot of eels worming in and out. But if the playing of jazz brings one extra smile into the world—go to it!"

And since jazz brought a lot of smiles to people's faces,

Sousa, with gnashing teeth, included it in his programs. The *Syncopators* had become a regular feature in his concerts, half an hour of jazz music which he called "Music of the Minute." And even though the last dance he had accepted had been the tango—he had written one himself in 1912—his fox-trotting granddaughter inspired him to a fox trot *Peaches and Cream*. A new Sousa march, a Sousa suite, a Sousa "humoresque," and a jazz potpourri—this was the basis of a typical Sousa program of the mid-twenties, or as one reviewer put it, the rack on which to hang encores.

Persuaded by public demand, Sousa could compromise with such abhorrent innovations as jazz and the phonograph. Yet he needed little urging to accept the movies. Actually, he loved them.

Every once in a while he would give his teen-age grandson and himself a special treat. John Philip Sousa, 3rd, would meet him at the Sousa Band office on Broadway, a bare room thick with cigar smoke, furnished with two battered desks and a large jar of hard candy. The two would lunch in the Republican Club and then take in a picture. They raved about *The Black Pirate* and Douglas Fairbanks, and dark-haired actresses who wore bangs.

In 1927 fans all over the nation celebrated Sousa's fiftieth anniversary as a conductor. Ignoring his haphazardous pursuits in this direction prior to 1877, he had set the official date of his conductorial debut at the time that he had given up playing in orchestras.

It had been suggested that Sousa write himself a Jubilee march. He would have done that for anyone else. And people could not understand why he refused.

"I have always been inspired by an occasion," he explained patiently. "Wherever my imagination was grasped by an event or a person I wrote a march. But I can't write a march on the Golden Jubilee of John Philip Sousa. I *can't!*"

And yet, inexorably, time took its toll.

Sousa marches were still selling. People still whistled them. But none of his later marches achieved the popularity of his old hits. His concerts no longer sold out. He had become an institution rather than an entertainer.

Radio executives tried every trick in the books to get Sousa on the air. Dr. Goldman who had a band program invited him to appear as his guest. But all that Sousa promised was to visit the studios as a sight-seer.

The Sousa family appeared in strength at NBC. Dr. Goldman showed them around. They watched a rehearsal led by Walter Damrosch. Sousa was baffled by the bustling of the young giant medium; he had never imagined that radio had developed so rapidly. But when someone pressed a baton in his hand and tried to make him conduct *The Stars and Stripes*, Sousa fled.

Two weeks later, he was knee-deep in preparations for his own radio program . . .

He was to conduct 52 selected bandsmen in a weekly show sponsored by General Motors. At 74 and a half years to the day he made his radio debut. Not only did he have a nation-wide audience; one of the hundreds of congratu · latory messages he received came from Commander Richard E. Byrd, then in the Antarctic.

Radio, Sousa found, made things easy. He had traveled enough—not one million miles, as it had been his goal, but nearly one and a half million, 60 times around the equator!

He had been heard and seen by an estimated 50 million people. He had spent some 15 million dollars on transportation and 13 million dollars in salaries.

He also had got around to golf. But he never did very well and would claim that the only game he ever won was against a youth who had never touched a club before.

On his seventieth birthday he had still been on the road; the cake had been cut in Cleveland. On his seventy-fifth birthday the country was benumbed by the impact of the stock-market disaster several days before.

On the day it happened, Sousa had come to town for his broadcast, and afterward dined at the St. Regis Hotel with his daughter Helen and several friends. Sousa, who had his sound investments and was no speculator, did not think the market crash a topic of particular interest. While gloom and despair settled over the nation's biggest city, Sousa and his party talked music and literature. Not one word of the catastrophe was said at the Sousa table.

Five months later, with the shadow of Depression looming, he introduced another of his great marches at the annual dinner of the Gridiron Club, in the presence of President Hoover and distinguished guests. *The Royal Welsh Fusiliers* commemorated the 30-year-old friendship between this famed ancient British regiment and the U. S. Marines, formed during the fight for Peking in the Boxer Rebellion.

chapter twenty-three

ON HIS seventy-seventh birthday, a slightly stooped and somewhat heavy Sousa conducted his band in the studios of WJZ. He posed for a picture cutting a huge birthday cake, played the indestructible *Stars and Stripes*, and told a nation-wide audience that he wanted to live to be a hundred so that he could write many more marches.

Many of his listeners had not yet been born when Sousa walked the wind-swept decks of the SS *Baltic*, worried about his business but inspired by the sight of the flag. But their patriotism was as strong as Sousa's and the old man's optimism was a comfort in a Depression-harassed period. If Sousa carried on despite his age, they would carry on despite all hazards. And the March King was not only delivering pep talks. He had composed seven more marches in 1931 and never canceled an engagement; and even though he avoided too strenuous commitments, his schedule was still remarkable.

On the eve of Lincoln's Birthday 1932, the New York Post of the American Legion awarded him an honorary citation as the oldest and most distinguished legionnaire; 50 members gave him a rousing ovation in the New York Athletic Club.

Eleven days later, in the capital, he led the combined

bands of the Army, Navy, and Marine Corps, on the occasion of Washington's two hundredth birthday. Enthusiastic crowds acclaimed their favorite musician and his newest opus, the *George Washington Bicentennial March*.

The piece had been written upon request of New York Congressman Sol Bloom, chairman of the Bicentennial Commission. With Sousa his band had come to Washington, and their reception indicated that they too were an American symbol. Captain Branson took the Marine Band to Union Station to greet the distinguished arrivals with a Sousa march. A motorcade, escorted by policemen on thunderous motorcycles, carried them up Pennsylvania Avenue, with gay flags fluttering from shiny vehicles, a modern version of parades of the past but as distinguished as ever. Then Sousa left his men and entered the White House grounds at the head of the Marine Band; on the south steps he conducted the *Bicentennial March* before President Hoover, the Bicentennial Committee, congressmen, and journalists who had turned out in no lesser strength than for crucial news conferences. Everybody listened with respectful appreciation to Sousa's new composition. Actually, the *Bicentennial* did not quite have the sparkle and vigor of some earlier marches; it was not Sousa at his best, yet it was unmistakable Sousa.

However, the concerts of Sousa's Band that afternoon and night were poorly attended, despite the escort and publicity the Marines had given it earlier in the day. The public at large was short of cash, and Sousa was not the latest fashion.

A few days later, on February 27, Sousa conducted the Marine Band at the Carabao "wallow," the annual meeting of the military order formed after the Spanish War. It was another fine craftsmanlike performance as there had been legion in the past and as there would be, almost everybody was certain, many more in the future.

The shadow of death had fallen over the path of many a friend and relative. His three brothers had gone, and only two of his sisters remained. But death had not shadowed him, and none of its messengers, frailty or unproductivity, had called. Only Sousa's podium, once almost two feet high, had gradually been cut down, until it measured five inches.

In 1931 doctors had discovered that a vertebra had been fractured in his riding accident nine years before; so strong were Sousa's powers of resistance that he had kept on for a decade with a broken neck.

He was chiefly surrounded by people who carried lighter burdens of years, yet came to him for support. He was in a hurry to leave Washington, where he usually was surrounded by nieces and nephews who were proud of "Uncle Johnny" who, besides being a celebrity, was so appreciative of the little things they had to offer that he would drive out to Chevy Chase for a dish of spaghetti made according to the family recipe. More important things, however, waited for him in New York.

ASCAP was fighting another crucial battle for a revision of the copyright law, and his advice was required as urgently as that of a chief of staff of an army locked in action. Sousa, as ASCAP's vice-president, was a very active executive, not just an honorary member. His associates on the committee—Sigmund Romberg, Gene Buck, Louis Froehlich, the lawyer—were youngsters as compared to him, men in their forties, to whom 56 years of protection seemed adequate. To this, Sousa objected. Fifty-six years to look forward to were a long period; but 56 years viewed from the vantage point of advanced age, were a brief span. All that was within the range of a man's recollection was brief. Sousa pleaded for perpetual copyright. He was thinking of great music that would endure forever.

He would not stay in New York either. On March 6 he was to conduct the Ringgold Band of Reading, Pennsylvania, on the occasion of its eightieth anniversary. He had guest-conducted this famed old organization on similar jubilees in the past.

On March 5 he was in Philadelphia. In the afternoon he went to see Dr. Cooke. "Do you believe in God?" he suddenly asked.

Dr. Cooke hastened to answer in the affirmative. "I'm glad you do," the bandmaster replied and smiled vaguely.

Abrupt as the question had come, it did not surprise Dr. Cooke. Sousa did not frequently talk religion, but his faith was deeply rooted and well known to his friends.

"I trust in God," he continued. "And the trouble with modernistic music of today is that it is written by men who don't believe in any kind of God. That is the reason why it will not last. Only *that* lasts which comes from God. These composers think that they do it themselves. Fools! They can acquire technique. They can learn the machinery of composition. They can build great musical structures, but they can't make living things. *They* are not alive. My music, my melodies, are not of my making; no matter how light, they came from a higher source. I have listened to a Higher Power."

Sousa went to the theater after dinner. *If Booth had missed* . . . The play fitted into his frame of mind. If that man had missed, if Lincoln had lived to a ripe old age, if

233

all crimes missed their targets—what would be the state of the world? But Fate determined hit and miss, and Fate was the Lord's prolonged arm. He sat through the performance no less absorbed in his own thoughts than in the production, and fascinated by both.

He could not go to sleep until the first shades of dawn floated through the blinds. In the morning, Dr. Cooke took him to Germantown to visit the Presser Home for Retired Music Teachers. They lunched at the Pennsylvania Athletic Club. Sousa was in a contemplative mood. Four times during the day he broached the subject of religion.

It was his firm belief that no music could survive that was not consecrated by faith in the Lord or had been composed in a godless land.

"A country without faith is a country without soul," Dr. Cooke later quoted him as having said. "Look at Russia. Is any music of great moment coming out of Russia now? Russia is chaos, and its music is chaos. Take a man's belief from him and at once his spirit starves."

Atheism and agnosticism were roots of many evils. Soul-searching and preoccupation with faith were only too appropriate in those days. The steady stream of national economy was badly hampered by depression. The hydra of crime raised another vicious head; Colonel Lindbergh's baby had been kidnaped a few days ago, and newspapers and radio were full with news of the tragedy.

The happy-go-lucky materialism of the twenties had been a delusion. Things material did not last forever. Spiritual values had to be resurrected to cope with fear and confusion. It was not for the first time that Sousa had seen his country cling to higher notions, as to a life belt in stormy waters. As long as the life belt of faith was at hand, America was safe.

They arrived in Reading at 6 P.M., Sousa with Marjorie Moody, his soloist, and Lillian Finegan, his secretary.

The Abraham Lincoln Hotel. The manes of the late President seemed to stay with him this week end—distant but never really remote memory of boyhood days. Sousa felt slightly weary. But he would not give in. He would start rehearsing at once. Nothing relieved fatigue so well as concentration.

The rehearsal was uneventful, but sufficiently stimulating to keep him fresh for the banquet in his honor afterward. He posed with Eugene Z. Weidner, the Ringgold Band's regular conductor, for a press photo. But while posing he felt the weariness again, and then he had to cough. He had several coughing spells during dinner; he would not take it seriously, there was nothing more trivial than that. But his voice was weak and his address short. He merely said that he wanted to marshal his strength for the concert, told two or three anecdotes, and sat down amid great applause.

The banquet guests wanted autographs. They stood in line, smiling, menus in hand, and Sousa wielded the pen, giving more than 100 signatures. His handwriting was firm, even though he once thought that his sight was blurred.

Fatigue . . . spring was in the air; everybody had spring fever every now and then, and spring made people cough and sniffle; a small price to pay for the finest season of the year.

He retired at 10:30 sharp. Miss Finegan accompanied him to his door and bade him a good night. She hoped fervently that he would rest. His cough had sounded . . . well, not really alarming but not quite harmless either, and Sousa did not look all too well—old, in fact . . . quite old . . .

Sousa had been anxious to be alone. His breath was not what it should be. All that talking and the smoke and the hustle and bustle of the banquet room; he actually felt a pressure on his chest, a slight pain—but once he got his collar off and could be alone, he would be all right.

His secretary next door heard him cough. She heard spells, some brief, some long. This was no common cold. She called at the door, inquired whether he needed anything. There was no reply.

Spells of coughing, and then yet another spell, wheezing, gasping, rattling . . . this was no manifestation of indisposition . . . this was the fading breath of a man struggling for his life . . .

A panting Sousa heard a rattling passkey; he saw Miss Finegan and a man. He did not quite know what she could want of him, nor who this man was who began to work on him. He was certainly in need of help, but he was not able to say exactly what he needed—they talked to him but he could not distinguish the words. He would have wanted to say something, but could not articulate . . . he was too weary for words, and there was that pressure on his chest, the choking and yet assuaging pain . . .

Sousa died at 1:30 A.M. on March 6, 1932, the family man, the squire of Port Washington, succumbing to a heart attack in a hotel room of a small town, attended by his secretary and a doctor he had never seen, away from his family and lifelong friends.

The funeral was to be held in Washington. Sousa's son-in-law rushed to Reading to supervise the transfer of the body. The widow and daughters were to go to the capital on March 7. John Philip, Jr., was on his way from La Jolla, California.

Only brief services took place in Reading, but several thousand people, including city officials and American Legionnaires, gathered, struck with sadness, as though a relative had passed away. The dead Sousa made them aware of their close association with the man who had given them *The Stars and Stripes*, *The Washington Post*, *Semper Fidelis*, and all those classics of an American philosophy expressed in tone and rhythm.

A blizzard struck. Snow changed into sleet and rain. It was the first heavy precipitation of a vanishing season. Through a lashing downpour a long, dark cortege marched to the station, behind the coffin covered with a soaked flag, the Ringgold Band playing *Nearer My God to Thee*, to the memory of a man who had believed that God stood by him as he composed himself into the hearts of men, many of whom had never seen him.

Four officers of the 123rd Coast Artillery Regiment provided a military escort on the train ride.

Snow fell in Washington when Sousa paid his final and permanent call. Dense flakes blanketed the city and piled smooth pillows over the steps and sidewalks on the way over which the flower-bedecked coffin was carried to the hearse. The snow hushed all sounds. No profane noises interfered with the March King's last ride.

In martial hustle and bustle, with proud fanfares, he had often led his musicians through Pennsylvania Avenue. It was but fitting that the man who would never march again should ride in serene silence through the old thoroughfare.

Lieutenant Commander Sousa would have been entitled to a military ceremony and a grave at Arlington. Authorities were prepared to give him a place of honor. But Sousa, the family man, had wanted to be laid to rest beside his parents, at Congressional Cemetery, close to his boyhood home.

Both Houses of Congress interrupted sessions for one minute of quiet remembrance of John Philip Sousa. Vice-President Charles Curtis was assigned to attend the funeral at the head of a senatorial delegation. In New York Leonard Liebling and Dr. Goldman went on the air to pay tribute to their great friend.

The body lay in state at the auditorium of the Marine Barracks, at the foot of the concert platform. Marines formed the guard of honor.

From the Botanical Gardens had come palms, lilies, roses, carnations, daffodils. They were piled up high behind the coffin of copper, and the Star-Spangled Banner was lovingly spread over its lower part. Worn battle flags on the walls lent a grim touch to the solemn splendor; some of those flags had once enraptured the youngster Philip who had watched the Grand Review.

No state funeral, no military pageant, could have been more solemn than the simple ceremony. Two Episcopalian ministers said brief prayers and, hidden behind the flowers, a quartet from the Gridiron Club sang hymns. From outside, where the flag on the parade ground was lowered to half-mast, came the strains of *Nearer My God to Thee*. Honorary pallbearers included high-ranking officers, Dr. Cooke, Dr. Goldman, Arthur Pryor, and a number of fellow townsmen from Port Washington. They carried the heavy coffin out of the auditorium near the parade ground which had witnessed the rise of a band-struck boy to a national figure; and at the gates, through which the boy had whisked many times, men presented arms.

Eight white horses pulled the hearse. Their red saddle cloth provided the only touch of color. A long file of automobiles followed. The snowfall had ceased. An intense cold gripped the city. Yet huge crowds lined the streets. The Marine Band played, starting with *El Capitan;* then, after one dirge, as Captain Branson had directed, they played *Semper Fidelis* all the short way to the cemetery. Motorcycle policemen cleared a path. Marines and sailors lined two sides of the grave and presented arms as the coffin was placed on its frame to the sounds of *Lead Kindly Light.* Priests said the commitment prayers. Freemasons placed an apron and sprigs of evergreen on the coffin. As the flag was removed, sailors fired three volleys. Taps were sounded as John Philip Sousa's remains were lowered into frozen earth.

epilogue

Jane van Middlesworth Bellis Sousa was 68 years old when her husband died, 14 months after they had celebrated their Golden Wedding Anniversary. She had been Mrs. Sousa throughout practically her entire adult life. They had been so much a part of each other that separation seemed inconceivable. Some friends wondered how she would carry on.

She carried on, for another 12 years, attended by her daughter Priscilla, surviving her son who succumbed to a heart attack in 1937. And she was still, first and above all, Mrs. John Philip Sousa, living symbol of a husband who had become a tradition.

She still wore the timeless, broad-brimmed hats she had worn in John Philip's day, and the pale blue or pink flowing gowns which he had preferred to current fashions. And whenever someone asked her, as interviewers almost invariably did, in what manner she had influenced her husband's career, the old lady would retort angrily that the great Sousa had never needed her or anyone else in the wide world to become what he had been.

Mrs. Sousa died in New York in 1944, in a world that seemed a different planet entirely from that into which she had been born. She was a beautiful woman to the last and acutely aware of the state of the world.

One century after his birth, Sousa is constantly remembered as a national figure, one of the uncontroversial great Americans.

The band's extensive library went to the University of Illinois; Sousa's favorite baton of light bamboo to Dr. Goldman, standard-bearer of band music, founder of the American Bandmaster's Association, of which Sousa had been the first president. Each November the various chapters of the Sousa Band Fraternal Society arrange memorial dinners in which surviving Sousa bandsmen and their families participate. ASCAP has established a John Philip Sousa Award for the best marches composed by military personnel. A bridge and a junior high school in Washington were named after him. But hardly ever will a memorial or monument express as clearly as his own words what he had aimed at and achieved.

"No one has had a richer, happier life than I have had. I believe that God intended me for a musician, and I was lucky that I could make my living by doing what I wanted to do. . . .

"America is a restless country. We do not want sadness. We want rhythm, and brightness . . . I have tried to put sunshine into music . . ."

Blessed was the life of a man who could say this shortly before his death.

bibliography

Bryan, Wilhelm B. *A History of the National Capital.* 2 vols. New York, Macmillan Co., 1914-1916.

Darlington, M. *Irish Orpheus.* Philadelphia, Olivier-Maney-Klein Co., 1950.

Darlington, William Aubrey. *The World of Gilbert and Sullivan.* New York, Crowell Co., 1950.

Gaisberg, Frederick. *The Music Goes Round.* New York, Macmillan Co., 1942.

Gerson, Robert A. *Music in Philadelphia.* Philadelphia, Theodore Presser Co., 1940.

Goldberg, Isaac. *The Story of Gilbert and Sullivan.* New York, Simon & Schuster, 1928.

Goldman, Dr. Edwin Franko. *Facing the Music.* Unpublished.

Goldman, Richard Franko. *The Band's Music.* New York, Pitman Co., 1938.

——. *The Concert Band.* New York, Rinehart & Co., 1946.

Graham, Alberta P. *Great Bands of America*. New York, Thomas Nelson & Sons, 1951.

Green, Abel and Laurie, Jr., Joe. *Show Biz*. New York, Henry Holt & Co., 1952.

Gurley, W. *Chicago World's Columbian Exposition*. Buffalo, Matthews Northrup Co., 1893.

Howard, John Tasker. *Our American Music*. New York, Crowell Co., 1939.

————. *Our Contemporary Composers*. New York, Crowell Co., 1941.

Howe, George Frederick. *Chester A. Arthur*. New York, Dodd, Mead & Co., 1934.

Jacob, H. E. *Johann Strauss, Father and Son*. New York, Greystone Press, 1940.

Johnson, R. (ed.). *A History of the World's Columbian Exposition Held in Chicago in 1893*. New York, Appleton & Co., 1898.

Jones, Robert W. *Journalism in the United States*. New York, Dutton & Co., 1947.

Kobald, Karl. *Johann Strauss*. Vienna, 1925.

Lummis, Charles F. *A Tramp Across the Continent*. New York, Scribner's, 1917.

McCabe, James D. *The Illustrated History of the Centennial Exhibition*. Philadelphia, Jones Bros. & Co., 1876.

Martin's World Fair Album. Chicago, 1893.

Martinet, André. *Offenbach, sa vie et son oeuvre*. Paris, 1887.

Miller, George. *The Military Band*. London, 1912.

Offenbach, Jacques. *Notes d'un musicien en voyage*. Paris, 1877.

244

Official Catalogue: *World's Columbian Exposition.* Chicago, 1893.

Pearson, Hesketh. *Gilbert and Sullivan.* New York, Har-
per & Bros., 1935.

Sousa, John Philip. *Marching Along.* Boston, Hale, Cush-
man & Flint, 1927.

Strauss, Eduard. *Erinnerungen.* Vienna, 1906.

Thomas, Rose Fay. *Memoirs of Theodore Thomas.* New
York, Moffat, Yard & Co., 1911.

Todd, Charles B. *The Story of Washington.* New York,
Putnam's Sons, 1893.

U. S. Library of Congress. Music Division. Bibliography
of the works of John Philip Sousa. Washington, 1935.

Wittemann, Adolph. *The World's Fair, Chicago, 1893.*
New York, Wittemann Co., 1893.

Contemporary newspapers and the following periodicals
were also consulted:

*Appleton's, The American Mercury, American Music
Journal, Current Literature, Etude, International Musi-
cian, Jacob's Orchestra Monthly, Metronome, Metropoli-
tan, Music, Musical America, Musical Courier, Musical
Observer, Musical Standard, Music Trade News, The
Saturday Evening Post, School Musician,* and *Tempo.*

index